LOOM
KNITTING
AFGHANS

LOOM
KNITTING
AFGHANS

20 SIMPLE & SNUGGLY NO-NEEDLE DESIGNS FOR ALL LOOM KNITTERS

ISELA PHELPS

ST. MARTIN'S GRIFFIN
NEW YORK

www.stmartins.com

Library of Congress Cataloging-in-Publication Data Available Upon Request

ISBN 978-1-250-04984-1

St. Martin's Griffin books may be purchased for educational, business, or promotional use. For information on bulk purchases, please contact Macmillan Corporate and Premium Sales Department at 1-800-221-7945 extension 5442 or write specialmarkets@macmillan.com

First U.S. Edition: June 2014

QTT.LKTC

This book was designed and produced by Quintet Publishing Limited
4th Floor, Sheridan House
114-116 Western Road
Hove BN3 1DD
UK

Photography: Lydia Evans
Illustrator: Bernard Chau
Designer: Tania Gomes
Project Editor: Julie Brooke
Art Director: Michael Charles
Managing Editor: Emma Bastow
Publisher: Mark Searle

10 9 8 7 6 5 4 3 2 1

Contents

Introduction

When my publisher contacted me about a possible afghan and throws book, my first thought went to the blanket that has been on my knitting loom for the past two years. I had a sudden panic attack and realized that accepting the project would mean facing one of my main challenges in my knitting life—finishing large projects! However, after our phone conversation, I kept thinking about the theme and how a knitted item of this magnitude would be the perfect way to demonstrate affection to our loved ones. The idea of demonstrating this love planted a seed in my heart and I wanted to be able to create a book that would allow us, loom knitters, a way to show our love and appreciation to our loved ones and even to ourselves. A group of sample loom knitters put all my project ideas to yarn and loom and this compilation of throws was born.

In this book, we have created a small bounty of blankets, afghans and throws. The projects range from easy baby blankets, double knit throws, to full-sized bed blankets. We have a little bit for everyone, simple beginner projects, intermediate designs with simple lace or colorwork, to advanced projects encompassing cables and lace. Each project gives you the opportunity to transfer loving thoughts to your loved one with each stitch.

We have included all the basic instructions on loom knitting and double knitting you will need to get started and the book also contains a breakdown of stitches. This particular feature breaks down difficult stitches into step-by-step instructions making it easier to create the stitch patterns.

It is my hope that you enjoy the projects in this book and find yourself inspired to pick up your knitting looms and yarn.

Happy looming,

Isela Phelps

Reading the patterns

Find all the materials and pattern information in the handy side bar. On the side bar, you will find the knitting loom needed, yarn, notions and even information on gauge.

Loom

Yarn

Gauge

Pattern style in this book

The patterns in the book are written in a short format to save on space and may look unfamiliar. Here is an example:

You will see:
CO 24sts, join to work in the round.
Work in 2x2 Rib stitch for 1 in (2.5 cm).
Work in st st until leg measures 6 in (15 cm) from CO edge.

It means:
Cast on 24 stitches/pegs. Connect the last stitch to the first stitch to prepare to knit in rounds.
Knit 2 stitches/pegs, purl 2 stitches/pegs, repeat the sequence around the loom until you reach the end of the round. Repeat the entire sequence until you have 1 in (2.5 cm) of work.
Switch to stockinette stitch (knit all rounds) and knit until you reach 6 in (15 cm) from the cast-on edge.

You will find a list of abbreviations on page 61.

Pattern presentation

*: used to mark the beginning of a repeated section.
You will see:
*K1, p1; rep from * to the end of row.

It means:
K1, p1, k1, p1, k1, p1.....

Projects for you to try

64 Entrelac Baby Blanket

68 Lace Baby Blanket

70 Cable Baby Blanket

74 Alphabet Baby Blanket

82 Stroller Stripes Blanket

88 Gentle Waves Baby Blanket

94 Ripple Lace Throw

96 Chevron Throw

98 Garter Stitch Afghan

100 Twist of Lime Cable Throw

104 Braid Circular Lapghan

106 Embossed Diamonds Throw

108 Aran Lapghan

110 Simple Afghan Throw

112 Just a Little Throw

PART ONE
Techniques & Materials

Using the loom

In knitting there are two schools of thought. In needle knitting, you have the Continental and English methods—in loom knitting we have the clockwise and counterclockwise methods.

In the clockwise school of thought, you will find yourself working around your knitting loom in a clockwise direction. Meaning, you will start knitting starting on the left side of the starting peg.

In the counterclockwise school of thought, you will find yourself working around the knitting loom in a counterclockwise direction. You will begin knitting on the peg to the right of your starting peg.

Both of the methods achieve the same goal. Choose the one that feels most comfortable to you. When working on the knitting loom, it doesn't matter which way you hold the knitting loom, with pegs facing you, or opposite you, or with the loom upside down. The knitting still looks the same.

A note of warning: when reading patterns, find out in which direction the pattern is worked. If you read the pattern in the wrong direction, you will end up with a mirror image of the design.

Most of the designs in this book are worked in a clockwise direction around the knitting loom.

Using the anchor peg

Some loom knitters prefer to use the anchor peg on their knitting loom to anchor their slip knot (see page 27). This is a small peg that appears at the side of the loom. If there isn't one you can use a thumbtack to secure the slip knot. To use the anchor peg when casting on, make a slip knot leaving a 5 in (12.5 cm) tail. Place the slip knot on the anchor peg on the side of your knitting loom. Perform Steps 2–5 on page 27 as before then remove the slip knot from the anchor peg.

Loom anatomy

There are some basic parts to the loom that you will become increasingly familiar with. This is a circular loom, but the elements are the same whether it is rake, board, or round.

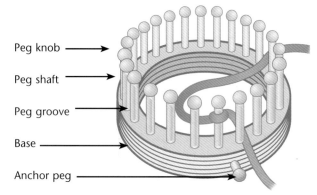

Peg knob

Peg shaft

Peg groove

Base

Anchor peg

NOTE ON THE TECHNIQUES

The techniques shown here are demonstrated on a circular loom, but the same principle is used for the looms used to knit large items, such as the blankets featured in this book.

Most of the techniques described in this chapter are used to make the blankets in the following chapters. You can use them to develop your loom-knitting skills and even create your own designs.

Knitting looms

The world of knitting looms continues to grow. At craft stores and online, you can now find a wide variety of knitting looms. If you are new to loom knitting it can be a daunting task finding the correct knitting loom for your project.

The majority of projects in this book were made on knitting looms with a large number of pegs to create a single panel. Each pattern will have the number of pegs needed for the project, as well as the gauge needed; we will also provide the exact knitting loom recommended for the project. However, each project can be worked on a different knitting loom so long as you have the correct number of pegs and gauge required.

Listed below are some of the knitting looms used in this book along with their characteristics. For more information see page 136.

Afghan Loom

Manufacturer: The Authentic Knitting Board Company

The Afghan Loom will provide you with the widest possible width amongst all the knitting looms presented in this section. Formed in an "S" shape to make it more portable and easier to work on while holding it on the lap, it has a regular gauge/sett and will produce a nice tight stitch with one strand of worsted weight yarn.

28-inch Knitting Board with Extenders

Manufacturer: The Authentic Knitting Board Company

This knitting loom is really versatile. It can produce single-sided knit fabric as well as double knit fabric. In this book, we have employed the versatility of this knitting loom to create double knit fabric. As the Afghan Loom above, it also has regular gauge/sett and worsted weight yarn is recommended for a tight stitch.

All-n-One Knitting Loom

Manufacturer: The Authentic Knitting Board Company

This knitting looms also provides good versatility. The knitter can produce single knit fabric as well as double knit. It is smaller than the 28-inch knitting loom making it more portable and easier to carry. The pegs are spaced at a small gauge/sett. Light worsted or DK weight yarn is recommended.

Knitting Boards

Double knit fabric is perfect for afghans and throws as it provides an item that looks perfect on both sides. The fabric created is thick and heavy, perfect for a cozy winter throw.

A knitting board is a knitting loom that has two rows of pegs facing each other. Weaving the yarn side to side on these two rows of pegs provides with a double-sided item.

The beauty of knitting board knitting lies on the final product—a reversible project!

Essential tools

The journey is about to begin and, like any journey, we need to gather our tools and gear up to make it easier and more enjoyable.

A knitting tool or pick

This is the most essential gadget for the loom knitter—you can never have enough of them. Keep a few on hand, or if you are obsessive like me, you will have a drawer full, as they are sneaky and tend to hide when you need them most.

The purpose of the knitting tool is to facilitate knitting on the loom. The tool allows you to lift the yarn up and over the peg, creating a stitch. A knitting tool is similar to a dental pick or nut pick; generally made out of metal, with a wood or plastic handle. The end is bent at an angle to allow you to lift off the stitches. Knitting tools come with different ends, some sharp for use when knitting on very small pegs and with fingering-weight yarns, some more blunt for use with bigger pegs and thicker yarns.

If you happen to lose all your knitting tools, you can also use a small crochet hook, nut pick, or even an orange peeler.

The yarn guide/aid

This is a thick plastic tube. It facilitates wrapping the yarn around the pegs and helps to maintain an even gauge in your wrapping. Some knitting loom vendors carry them as part of their line; if you are unable to find one, you can easily make one (see box below).

A stitch and gauge guide

This allows you to determine exactly the number of stitches and rows per 1 in (2.5 cm) in your work. It is a piece of flat metal or plastic with ruler markings on the sides. In the center there is a small L-shaped window that allows you to check the rows and stitches per 1 in (2.5 cm) of the knitted piece. If you don't have one, you could make one out of stiff cardboard.

To check the gauge, block the knitted piece lightly, place it on a flat surface, then place the stitch gauge guide on top of it. Line the bottom cut-out window opening with one row of the knitted piece and one of the columns of stitches to the side (see page 34). To determine the gauge, count the stitches per 1 in (2.5 cm) in the window opening. Count also the rows per 1 in (2.5 cm). Make sure to count quarter stitches and half stitches.

Scissors/yarn cutters

These are invaluable. Some yarns are easy to break with your hands; however, you will find that many synthetic

How to make a yarn guide

- Find a Bic-style ballpoint pen with a hollow center.

- Take out the inside ink cartridge.

- Cut the tip off the barrel.

- Sand any rough spots with an emery board and it is ready to use.

- Pass the starting tail of the yarn through and wrap around the pegs with the aid of your new yarn guide.

No pens around? No problem. Get a thick drinking straw. Cut it so you have a piece that is about 5 in (12.5 cm) long. Thread your yarn through it and you are ready to start wrapping your yarn around the pegs.

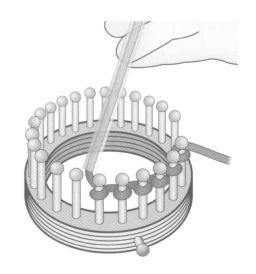

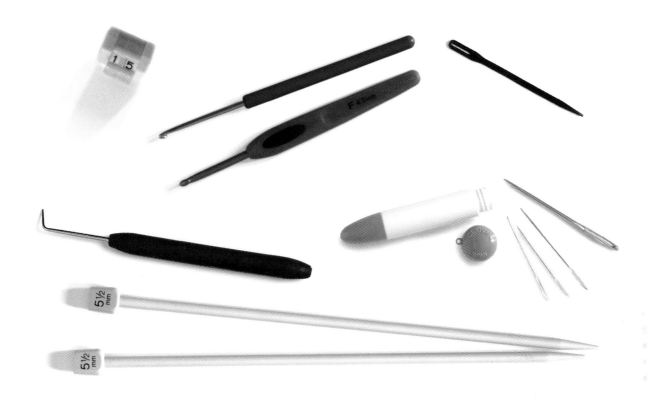

yarns and cottons are almost impossible to break. Carrying small scissors in your knitting bag is always advisable. If traveling by airplane, I recommend obtaining a yarn/thread cutter that you can take along with you.

A row counter

This is a nifty item to have in your knitter's bag. It comes in handy … as long as you don't forget to change the setting. Row counters come in various shapes: cylindrical, square, and circular. There are two types of cylindrical row counters. One of them has an opening that is usually used to insert a knitting needle through; in our case it can be fitted over the knitting tool. The second one has a small ring attached to one of the sides that allows you to put it over a peg and keep it at the base of the knitting loom. The square and circular types are mechanical in that you only need to push a button to increase the numbers.

Although all of them help in keeping track of rows, you have to remember to reset them at the beginning of each section.

Crochet hooks

These are very useful. Don't worry, crochet knowledge is not necessary to loom knit, unless you want to crochet an edging around your knits. Crochet hooks just come in handy when picking up a dropped stitch or when casting off a flat panel from the knitting loom. It is advisable to have the size of crochet hook called for on the yarn label, as this will make it easier to handle the yarn. In general, carrying a medium-size hook in your knitting bag will suffice.

Single-pointed knitting needles

Don't run, wait! You won't be using them to knit. There, you can relax! The needles are only going to be used as stitch holders.

I would recommend obtaining a pair of US size 8 (5 mm) and a pair of US size 2 (2.75 mm). The US size 8 (5 mm) can be used with the large and regular gauge looms, while the US size 2 (2.75 mm) can be used with the smaller gauges.

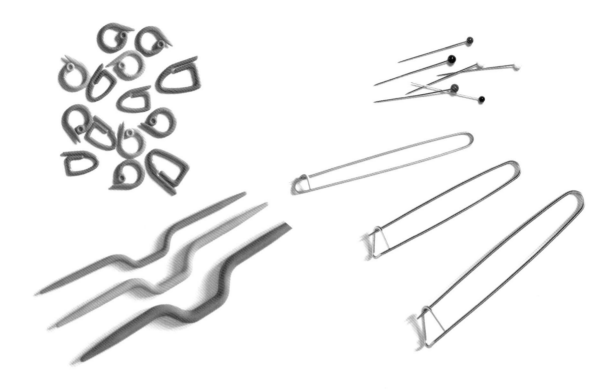

Tapestry needles

These are used for seaming the sides of a knitted garment, for gathering and closing the ends of hats, and for weaving in the ends on the knitted garment. Tapestry needles are made from plastic or metal. They have a larger eye than regular sewing needles. The plastic needles are flexible and you can bend them. The metal needles are smoother and won't snag the knitted item. Both styles of needles have blunt ends that prevent the yarn splitting. As with the crochet hooks, the needles come in different sizes, and the eye opening will fit certain thickness of yarns; it is advisable to have a collection of needles with different-size eye openings.

Pins

These have uses everywhere in the knitting world; they can turn a curled piece of stockinette into a nice straight sleeve. They are essential tools in the finishing of knitted pieces. The straight pins with colored heads are perfect to use when seaming two sides together. Large T-pins make blocking a knitted garment a breeze. These pins can be found at any yarn shop. Do not use any other household pin as it may rust and leave marks on your knits.

Stitch holders

These look like oversize safety pins, except they have a blunt end. They are useful for holding live stitches that will be worked on later in the project, such as a neckline or a tricky bit of shaping. They come in different sizes and it is advisable to have an array of sizes in your knitting bag. Small coil-less safety pins also come in handy when holding only a few stitches or marking the right or reverse side of a knitted item.

Stitch markers

These are small rings that can be used to mark the pegs where special stitches or other special treatments need to be done on the knitted item. Usually, the stitch markers are used on knitting needles. However, since they are small rings, they fit perfectly over the pegs on a knitting loom and can sit at the base of the loom to remind the loomer that the peg has a stitch that requires special treatment.

Split ring stitch markers are very helpful in marking a stitch itself rather than the peg. The open split rings are removable by simply opening the ring and sliding it off the peg. They come in various shapes, sizes and colors. Having a variety of different colors is recommended.

Measuring tape or ruler

This is a loom knitter's best friend; no knitting bag should be without at least one. When choosing a good measuring tape, choose a material that won't distort easily. Discard any tape at the first sign of wear, even if it's your favorite. A distorted measuring tape can spell disaster for your knitted garment as it won't measure accurately. It is also advisable to have a small plastic ruler on hand.

Cable needles

These come in different shapes and sizes. They are available in plastic and metal. Usually, one package contains three different sizes; choose the size that best works with the yarn in a project.

Until very recently, loom knitters were not able to create cables on a knitting loom, as the nonelasticity of the stitches set on the knitting loom made it difficult. However, this has changed. Now we are able to create cables and have added the use of cable needles to our extensive gadget repertoire.

Calculator

Yep, you read it right, we will still be doing math. I know you thought math was long gone with school, but it has come to haunt you again; and it wants to be your best friend. No worries, though; you can cheat this time and use a calculator. It will come in very handy when calculating gauge or even adding a few pegs to the count in the pattern.

Other equipment

Sticky notes

Stickies are a great way to mark the row on the paper pattern you are knitting. After knitting each row, move the note down the page. There are two schools of thought about sticky notes: Cover the previous knitted row and expose the rows to come. Cover the future rows and only expose the rows worked on. It is up to you to decide which method works best for you.

Notebook

A place to jot down ideas about the patterns, comments about yarns, and other loomy gems.

Ball winder

This little gadget allows you to wind your yarn into an easy-to-use center-pull ball. Two styles are available, manual and electric, but you can always make balls the old-fashioned way with your hands.

Yarn swift

A yarn swift is usually used in conjunction with the ball winder. It resembles the inside of an umbrella. It holds a hank of yarn while you wind it into a ball. When used along with the ball winder, the yarn swift unwinds the hank of yarn and the ball winder winds it into a ball. If you don't have one of these, persuade a passerby to sit still with his or her arms outstretched while you wind your ball, or failing that, use the back of a chair.

Fingernail file/emery board

Is your yarn catching on the pegs? Some knitting looms have small burs on the pegs that may snag the yarn. Use the emery board to sand down the small burs and you have smooth looming ahead!

Knitting bag

You need a bag that is big enough to hold your project and your knitting loom and sturdy enough to carry the weight of the knitting loom. The bag should have a comfortable handle to hold or carry around, and have pockets, lots of pockets to put in all the yummy gadgets and notions, and even a small snack for the reward moments. If possible, it should be waterproof so if it happens to rain, your knitting is safe. Closures should be either zippers or buttons; say no to Velcro—this will snag your yarn and can even destroy your knitted item if caught.

Yarn 101: a quick refresher on yarn

One of the perks of any fiber art is the luxurious yarn "needed" for the projects. The market is saturated with luscious, soft, sparkly yarns, which vary in color, texture, and fiber content.

Consider this a crash course on yarn. Before going all out and purchasing ten skeins of that pretty yarn you fell in love with, let's take a small trip to the yarn store and get personal with the yarns.

Feel them close to your skin; the neck or the inside of your forearm are good places to see how your skin reacts to the properties of the fiber. Check the color in different lighting and move around the yarn store to see the effect that different lighting has on the yarn. If possible, ask if you can see it outside under daylight. Pull at it to test its elasticity; some yarns have more elasticity than others and this can affect the overall look of the project.

Check the yarn label for important fiber-related information. The label contains essential information, such as fiber content, color, dye lot (if any), washing instructions, and yardage. Keep the yarn labels of any project until you have completed it. Recently, a friend of mine moved to a different state at the same time she was knitting a beautiful Fair Isle scarf and she ran out of one of the colors. Fortunately, she had saved the label and was able to match the exact dye lot at a different yarn store in her new location. Moral of the story: keep your yarn labels.

Yarns come wound in different shapes: cones, skeins, hanks, and balls. A cone has a cardboard center that has yarn wound around it. Its starting tail is on the inside of the cone. Reach your hand into the cone, and pull out the center. If lucky, you will find the starting tail right away. A ball is ready to use and usually has a starting tail in the center. Once you start loom knitting, do not stop until you have finished knitting all the yarn you took out from the center, or make sure to wind it loosely round the outside of the ball. A hank is a loosely wound coil of yarn held together by a string at two sides of the coil. A skein is the hank twisted into a manageable shape, and you will need to wind a hank or skein into a ball. Yarns are divided into two groups: natural and synthetic fibers. Under natural yarns, there are two subdivisions: protein- and cellulose-based.

Protein-based fibers

These are the most well known and include wool, angora, cashmere, mohair, and alpaca. Protein fibers such as wool are popular among loom knitters for their warm, elastic, and durable characteristics. Wool is known as a good all-year-round fiber.

Cellulose-based fibers

Cotton is the most widely known vegetable/cellulose fiber. Known for its cooling properties, cotton is often used for summer garments as it absorbs moisture and dries quickly, although it does not have the elasticity of wool. Another natural fiber, silk, is known for its smoothness and softness. To provide elasticity or warmth, yarn manufacturers often mix these natural yarns with other fibers to benefit from the properties they lack.

Synthetics

Synthetics have opened the door to a fun world of novelty yarns—think funky, sparkly, nubby textured yarns. Synthetic yarns have the great advantage of being machine-washable, making them a great choice for children's loom knits. However, synthetics are hot and have little or no absorbing properties, and can leave the wearer feeling as if they just came out of a steam room session. Manufacturers often combine synthetics with other fibers to achieve certain qualities that other fibers may lack.

Yarn weights

Yarns come in different thicknesses, known as weights. The thicker the yarn, the bigger the stitches made. Yarn weights range from fine to bulky. The finer the yarn, the closer the pegs need to be on the knitting loom. The table above gives a standard reference guide for yarn and its use on knitting looms. So many yarns, so little time! Choosing the right yarn for the project can be a little daunting when starting on the journey.

Variegated-color yarns

These work best with simply stockinette stitch or other simple stitch patterns that will allow the beauty of the colors to show. Textured stitches will be hard to see through the color changes.

Solid-color yarns

Recommended for cables or any other stitch patterns. Cables show better with light color yarns.

Novelty yarns

Think simple stockinette or garter stitch to show off the special characteristics of the yarn; anything more complex won't show. Once you have chosen the yarn for your project, knit up a small swatch and wash it a couple of times. Check for the following: colorfastness, pilling, drape, shrinkage, and most importantly, does it show the stitch pattern as you imagined it?

Yarn weight

Yarn Weight Symbol & Category Names	0 LACE	1 SUPER FINE	2 FINE	3 LIGHT	4 MEDIUM	5 BULKY	6 SUPER BULKY
Type of Yarns in Category	Fingering 10–count crochet thread	Sock, Fingering, Baby	Sport, Baby	DK, Light Worsted	Worsted, Afghan, Aran	Chunky, Craft, Rug	Bulky, Roving
Knit Gauge Range* in Stockinette Stitch to 4 in (10 cm)	33–40** sts	27–32 sts	23–26 sts	21–24 sts	16–20 sts	12–15 sts	6–11 sts
Recommended Loom Gauge	EFG	EFG–FG	FG	ESG	SG–RG	LG	ELG

EFG =Extra Fine Gauge

FG =Fine Gauge

ESG =Extra Small Gauge

SG =Small Gauge

RG =Regular Gauge

LG =Large Gauge

ELG =Extra Large Gauge

Casting on

The foundation row for loom knits is called the cast-on row, abbreviated as CO. Every cast-on method starts with a slip knot (see page 27).

The e-wrap cast on (CO)

This cast on is called the e-wrap because if you look at it from an aerial view it resembles cursive e's. Use the e-wrap cast on when the first row needs to be picked up for a brim or seam or the cast-on row needs to be extremely flexible.

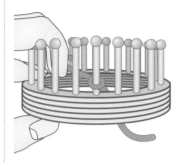

1 Place a stitch marker on any of the pegs on the knitting loom. This will be your starting peg. Make a slip knot, and place it on the peg with the stitch marker.

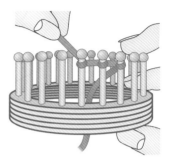

2 With the working yarn in your left hand, * pull the working yarn toward the inside of the loom, wrap around the peg directly to the left counterclockwise. * Repeat from * to *.

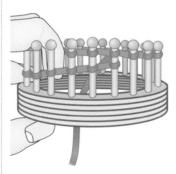

3 Wrap each peg a second time in the same method. Each peg should have 2 loops on it. Hold the working yarn in place so the wraps do not unravel.

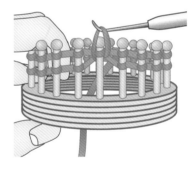

4 Insert the tip of knitting tool on the bottommost loop on the last peg wrapped. Lift the loop up and off the peg (knitting over, KO) and allow the loop to fall toward the inside of the knitting loom. Go to the left and repeat.

Cable cast on

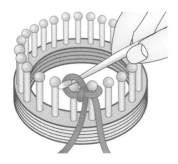

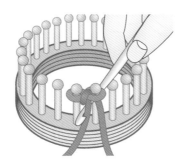

1 Place a slip knot on the first peg on the loom. Take the working yarn to the outside of the loom. With a crochet hook, insert the tip of the hook through the slip knot and hook the yarn, forming a loop. Place the loop on the adjacent peg to the left.

2 With the crochet hook go below the traveling yarn, hook the working yarn and pull toward the inside and toward the third peg. Place the loop from the hook on the next adjacent peg. Repeat this all around the loom.

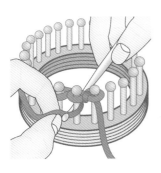

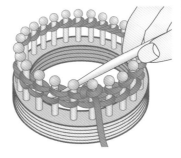

3 When you reach the last peg, place the loop on the first peg. The front of each peg has 2 loops, while the inside only shows 1. E-wrap the first peg with the working yarn. Knit over the 2 lowest strands, leaving only 1 loop on the peg.

4 Knit over the bottommost loop on all the remaining pegs on the loom. Loom is ready to be worked in desired pattern stitch. This creates a neat, non-loopy, thick cable-like flexible edge that is good for hats.

Slip knot

1 Fold the circle over the working yarn that is coming from the ball.

2 Reach through the circle, and grab the yarn coming from the skein.

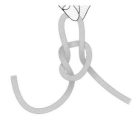

3 Pull the working yarn through circle, while also pulling gently on the short end of the yarn tail end, thus tightening the noose on the knot. Slip knot completed.

Chain cast on

1 Form a slip knot with your yarn. Insert crochet hook through slip knot with the hook toward the center of the knitting loom and the working yarn on the outside of the loom.

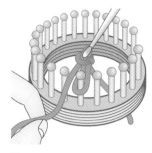

2 Place hook between first two pegs. Hook the working yarn and pull the working yarn through the slip knot that is on the crochet hook (thus, wrapping the post of the peg).

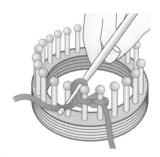

3 With crochet hook toward the inside of the loom, move up between the next set of pegs (between the second and third peg) and repeat Step 2, continuing all around the loom.

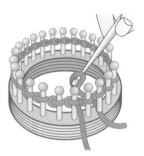

4 When you reach the last peg, take the loop on the hook and place it on the first peg. Knitting loom is ready to be knitted on.

Board cast on

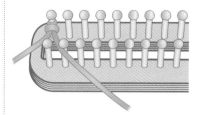

1 Make a slip knot and place it on the first top peg of the knitting board. Take working yarn down to the next peg along, and opposite, and wrap around it.

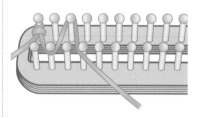

2 Go back again, missing another peg, wrap around, then down to the fourth peg, wrap around it. Continue in this manner, skipping every other peg, until you reach the end of the board (or the number of stitches you want to cover for your pattern).

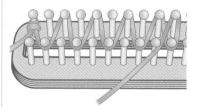

3 To complete the cast on, go to the peg directly across, wrap it. Continue wrapping the pegs that were skipped in Steps 1 and 2.

Long tail cast on

This is known as the long tail cast on because you use the tail of the yarn and the working yarn to create the cast on. This term is also used in needle knitting. It creates a flexible cast on.

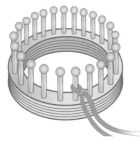

1 Make a slip knot, leaving a tail that is about four times as long as the width of your project. Place the slip knot on a peg. The slip knot will become your first stitch.

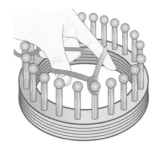

2 Position your left hand palm down: wrap the working yarn around your index finger and the tail over your thumb. Hold both yarn ends with the remaining three fingers.

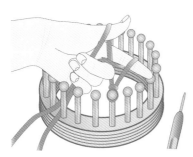

3 Flip your hand toward the left until your palm faces up. The hand is now in a slingshot position.

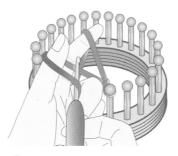

4 Guide a crochet hook by the palm side of the thumb under the yarn strand, then guide it over to the yarn strand on the index finger, hook the yarn strand on the index finger, and guide it down through the loop on your thumb.

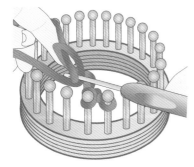

5 Place the loop on the adjacent empty peg. Remove your thumb from its loop and gently tug on the yarn tail to tighten the new stitch that you created. Repeat Steps 3–5 until you have the number of stitches called for in the pattern.

No crochet hook?

There is a method of using the long tail cast on without a crochet hook but it is slightly more complicated.

1 With the slip knot on your first peg, grab the tail yarn and e-wrap the peg to the left. The peg now has two loops. Knit over so only one loop remains.

2 Grab yarn coming from the skein and e-wrap the next empty peg.

3 Grab the tail yarn and place it above the e-wrap completed in Step 2. Lift the bottom loop over and off the peg (the peg should remain wrapped with the tail).

4 Repeat Steps 2 and 3 with the remaining pegs.

TIPS

● You may find it more comfortable to place the loom on your lap or a table to work the cast on.

● When making your slip knot, it is better to overestimate and make the tail too long rather than too short.

Binding off

Used at the end of a project to bind off all the stitches, as well as when you have to bind off certain amount of stitches for buttonholes, armhole shaping, necklines, and other openings. Binding off prevents stitches from unraveling.

Basic bind off

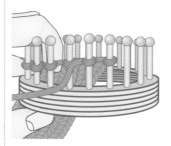

1 Knit two stitches (pegs 1 and 2).

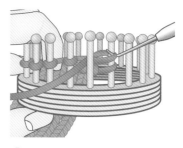

2 Move the loop from the second peg over to the first peg. Knit over.

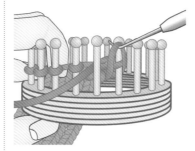

3 Move the loop on the first peg over to the peg just emptied.

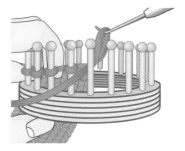

4 Knit the next peg. Repeat Steps 2–4 until you have bound off the required number of stitches. A stitch will remain on the last peg. Cut the yarn leaving a long tail. E-wrap the peg and knit over—pull the tail end through the stitch.

Yarn over bind off

The yarn over bind off provides a stretchy border, perfect for items that require a flexible opening.

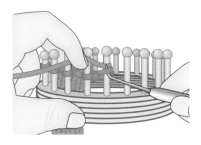

1 Knit the first stitch (peg 1).

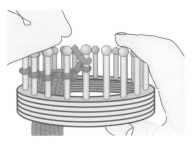

2 Wrap the peg in a clockwise direction, knit over.

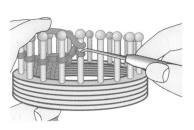

3 Knit the next stitch (peg 2).

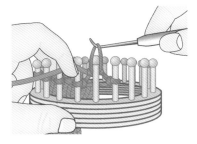

4 Move the stitch over (from peg 2 to peg 1) to the peg on the left. KO. Repeat Steps 2–4 until all the stitches required have been bound off. A stitch will remain on the last peg. Cut the working yarn leaving a 5 in (12.5 cm) tail. E-wrap the peg and knit over—pull the tail end through the stitch.

Single crochet bind off

1 Remove a stitch from the peg with the hook (2 loops on hook). Wrap the working yarn round the crochet hook.

2 Pull the yarn through the loops on the hook to make another loop.

3 Move to the next peg and repeat Steps 1–2. When you reach the last stitch, cut the working yarn leaving a 5 in (12.5 cm) tail, hook the tail and pass it through the last stitch to lock it in place.

Double crochet bind off

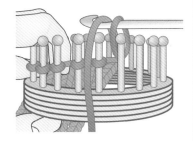

1 Hook the working yarn with the crochet hook; pull the yarn through the stitch on the hook to make a loop.

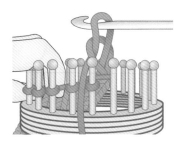

2 Make 1 chain (crochet 1 chain). Move to the next peg and repeat Steps 1–2.

3 When you reach the last stitch, cut the working yarn leaving a 5 in (12.5 cm) tail, hook the tail and pass it through the last stitch to fasten off.

Sewn bind off

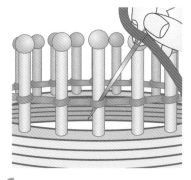

1 Pass the needle through the first stitch by inserting the needle from top to bottom.

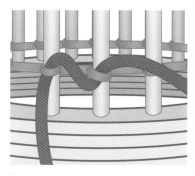

2 Pass the needle through the second stitch by inserting the needle from top to bottom.

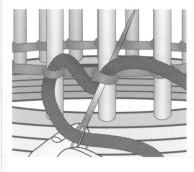

3 Insert the needle through the first stitch by inserting the needle from bottom to top.

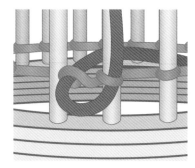

4 Take the stitch off the peg. Repeat Steps 1–4 until there is only one stitch on the loom. Pass the needle through the stitch from bottom to top. Take stitch off the peg.

Joining two panels by binding off

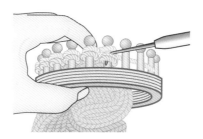

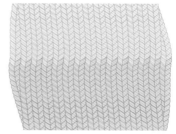

1 Place one of the panels on the knitting loom with the right side facing the inside of the knitting loom; the wrong side will be facing you. Pay close attention to putting the stitches back on the knitting loom correctly.

2 Place the second panel on the knitting loom by placing the stitches on the same pegs that the first panel is occupying, right sides of the panels together. Follow the basic bind off method (see page 30) and bind off the stitches—knit through both stitches on the pegs.

3 Take the two stitches off the peg and place the newly formed loop on the peg. Once you get the hang of this, your seams will be invisible.

Gauge

Let's take a small break and look at some numbers. Don't be scared and run away, but do feel free to reach for a little chocolate to calm your nerves. It's not algebra, honest.

When working on blankets and throws gauge is not imperative, as the item does not need to fit a specific individual. However, you will need to recalculate the amount of yarn needed if your gauge does not match that of the designer. Let's create a swatch and find out how to check the gauge.

Make a Sample Swatch

To loom-knit a swatch, cast on the same number of stitches as called for in the gauge section of the pattern plus 10 more. If the gauge for the pattern states 4 stitches over 2 in (5 cm), then cast on 14 stitches. Loom-knit the swatch on the stitch pattern used in the pattern until it reaches about 6 in (15 cm) in length, then bind off.

To measure for gauge, count all stitches—remember quarter and half stitches count! Measure in a few different places to make sure that the gauge is consistent. Remember that Stitch Gauge Guide in the tools section (page 20)? Well, it's time to take it out for a spin. If you don't have one, you can also use a measuring tape.

Knit a small swatch to try out the stitches. Set it on a flat surface. Set your stitch guide in the center of your swatch. Align your stitch guide so that a row is aligned with the horizontal part of the L-shaped window. Count

the number of stitches along the horizontal side of the window. Write the number down. Now, count the rows along the vertical side of the window. Write down the number. The numbers are your gauge for that loom, using the type of yarn in the project, and the stitch used in the project. In this diagram, for example, there are 10 stitches across and 19 rows.

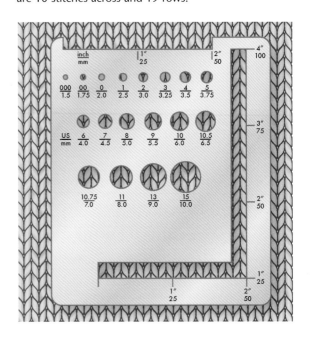

Got gauge?

You can go forth and start loom knitting! Count yourself lucky.

More stitches?

If you have more stitches per 1 in (2.5 cm) than called for in the pattern, what does this mean? It means that if you go forth and knit with this yarn and loom, then the item may be too small. Try a thicker yarn or a larger-gauge knitting loom.

Fewer stitches?

If you have fewer stitches per 1 in (2.5 cm) than called for in the pattern, what does this mean? It means that if you are stoic enough to continue, you will end up with an item that may be big enough to fit Goliath! Try a thinner yarn or a smaller gauge knitting loom.

Gauge is dependent upon four factors

- Yarn
- Gauge of the knitting loom
- Type of stitch
- Your personal wrapping gauge

The first three elements will have the most impact upon gauge. If any of these three elements change, the gauge will change.

Playing with numbers

If your heart is still set on a specific yarn but you still don't get gauge, don't despair: you can still continue. Bring out the calculator, do some math and calculate the number of stitches and rows you will need to create the same item.

Let's assume you want to knit a square that is 20 x 20 in (50 x 50 cm). The gauge given in the pattern is 6 stitches and 8 rows in 2 in (5 cm). To create the square with the gauge above you will need to cast on 60 stitches and knit for 8 rows. But your swatch tells you that you've got a gauge of 4 stitches and 6 rows in 2 in (5 cm). To create the square of 20 x 20 in (50 x 50 cm) you will need to make the following changes: cast on 40 pegs and knit 60 rows.

I know it is a bit frustrating knitting swatches but it is worth taking the time to knit a small swatch. Don't look at your swatches as lost time or yarn. You can always make something from them. Make small bags by knitting a rectangular swatch, folding it in half and seaming the sides of the rectangle with mattress seam stitch. Knit a long I cord, attach it to the bag and ta-da! Your swatch became a little bag.

Left: Each stitch affects the gauge differently. For instance, the single stitch here has slightly lopsided Vs and will create a different gauge to any other you might choose.

Basic stitches

Single stitch (ss)

This is the simplest stitch to get you started. Wrapping the entire loom and then knitting over may be quicker, but can create a ladder effect between the first and last peg. Also, since you are knitting in the round, if you wrap all the pegs then knit them over, your item will have a tendency to twist and you will see your vertical lines of stitches spiral around the item.

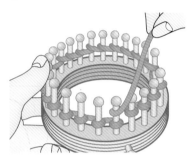

1 To create the single stitch, just e-wrap around all the pegs on the loom.

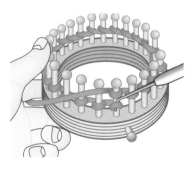

2 "Knit over" by lifting the bottom loop up and off the peg as shown.

There are three different ways to work a knit stitch: knit stitch is a taller and wider stitch; flat stitch is short and narrow; U stitch is medium height and width.

Knit stitch (k)

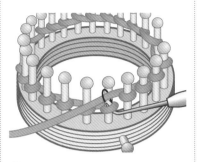

1 Insert the knitting tool through the stitch on the peg from bottom up.

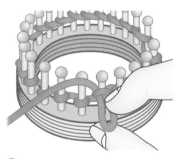

2 Hook the working yarn with knitting tool, making a loop. Grab the loop with your fingers.

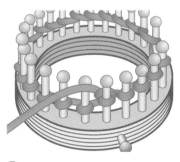

3 Take the original loop off the peg and replace with the new. Gently tighten the working yarn. Repeat Steps 1–3 to complete a knit row.

Purl stitch (p)

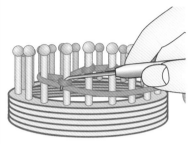

1 Insert the knitting tool from top to bottom through the stitch on the peg and scoop up the working yarn with the knitting tool.

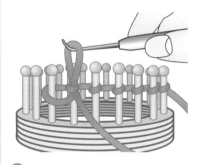

2 Pull the working yarn through the stitch on the peg to form a loop. Hold the new loop with your fingers.

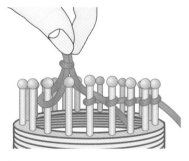

3 Take the old loop off the peg and place the new loop on the peg. Tug gently on the working yarn to tighten the stitch. Repeat Steps 1–3 to complete a purl row.

Double stitch (ds)

This is also known as the one-over-two. The knitting loom needs to be prepped with three loops on each peg and the bottommost loop on the peg is lifted over and off the peg. This produces a tighter stitch than the single stitch. It also resembles the twisted knit stitch.

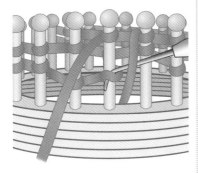

1 Cast on your knitting loom. E-wrap all around the knitting loom one more time. Each peg has two loops on each peg.

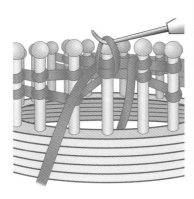

2 E-wrap the first peg, which now has three loops. Knit over by picking the bottommost strand off the peg (two loops remain). Repeat Step 2 all around the loom until you reach the last peg. As you move to the next peg, you may have to push down the wraps on the peg to fit the third wrap on the peg. The pegs will always have two loops after being knitted over.

Half stitch (hs)

The half stitch is so named as you have to e-wrap around the loom four times, then, knit-over two over two. It produces a thicker stitch than the double stitch. As the single stitch, and the double stitch, the knitting will resemble the twisted knit stitch. If you are knitting with a thin yarn on a large-gauge knitting loom, you may want to use the half stitch.

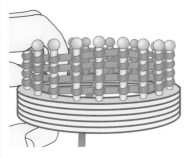

1 Cast on your knitting loom. E-wrap all around the knitting loom three more times. Each peg has four loops.

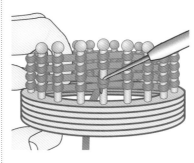

2 Knit over by lifting the lower two strands off the peg. Repeat all around the knitting loom. Each of the peg remains with two loops.

Flat stitch (fs)

This variation looks exactly like the knit stitch, except it is shorter and tighter.

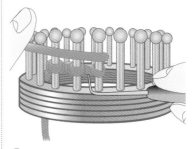

1 Take the working yarn to the front of the peg and place it above the loop on the peg. Do not place any gauge on it; simply rest it above.

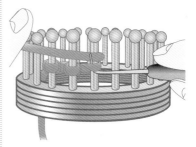

2 Insert the tool through the loop.

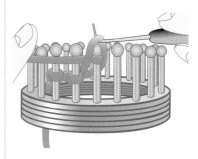

3 Lift the loop off the peg.

U-stitch (u-st)

This variation looks exactly like the knit stitch, except that it is shorter and tighter. However, it is a little bigger and not as tight as the flat stitch.

  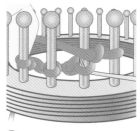 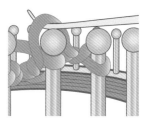

1 Take the working yarn to the front of the peg and place it above the loop on the peg.

2 Wrap the working yarn around the peg, as if hugging the peg with the yarn.

3 Insert the knitting tool through the loop on the peg.

4 Lift the loop off the peg.

Advanced stitches

Chunky braid stitch (cbs)

This stitch resembles a knitted braid. It is also known as the three-over-one stitch, or braid stitch. It produces a thick, nonstretchy fabric with a very tight stitch. If you are knitting with a thin yarn, you may want to try this stitch throughout your project to get a firm stitch.

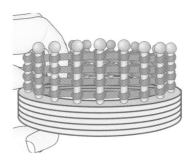 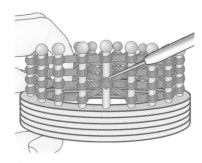

1 Cast on your knitting loom. E-wrap all around the knitting loom three more times. Each peg should now have four loops.

2 Knit over by lifting the bottommost three loops off the peg. Repeat the knitting-over process all round the loom. The pegs remain with one loop each.

Twisted knit stitch

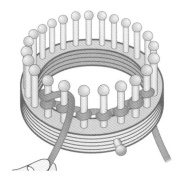

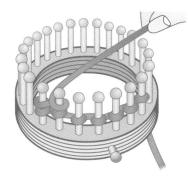

1 E-wrap the last peg in a counterclockwise direction, run the working yarn behind to the next peg and wrap around it in a clockwise direction. Knit over this stitch, then go back and knit over on the first peg. Tug on the yarn gently to tighten the first stitch.

2 Continue knitting back to the next pegs in a clockwise direction. When you reach the last peg on the right, knit it, then bring working yarn to the front of the peg. Wrap around it in a clockwise direction. Bring working yarn behind the pegs.

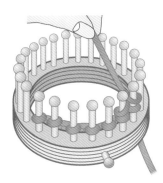

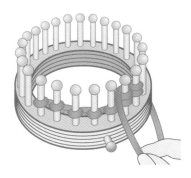

3 E-wrap the next peg in a counterclockwise direction. Knit over. Go back to the first peg and knit the stitch. Tug gently on the working yarn to tighten the first stitch.

4 Continue knitting down the loom, e-wrapping the pegs in a counterclockwise direction.

Using twisted stitches and mock cables for texture

The principle of twisting stitches to create texture consists of two stitches changing places. No special tools are necessary as it is not strictly a cable, rather a mock cable. Every time stitches are crossed over one another, the knitted item shrinks horizontally—twisting stitches makes the knitted piece narrower. Most of the time, you will encounter twisted stitch patterns on a background of reverse stockinette. The background of purl stitches helps bring out the twisted stitches and give them a three-dimensional appearance.

How to twist the stitches for right slanting: Take stitch from peg 3 off the knitting loom, hold it on your knitting tool, or on a cable needle, place it toward the center of the knitting loom. Move stitch from peg 4 to emptied peg 3. Place the stitch from the cable needle on peg 4.

How to twist the stitches for left slanting: Take stitch from peg 4 off the knitting loom, hold it on your knitting tool, or on a cable needle, place it toward the center of the knitting loom. Move stitch from peg 3 to emptied peg 4. Place the stitch from the cable needle on peg 3.

Cables

A cable is a design feature that creates a ropelike twist in the knitting. The twist is created by placing a few stitches on hold on a cable needle, so that the stitches may be worked out of their usual order. Although cables may seem a bit intimidating at first, with practice you will notice that they are quite simple. Cables work best when worked with yarns that have some inherent elasticity—for instance yarns with wool content. Use a cable needle or a double-pointed knitting needle to hold your stitches while you cross them. When creating a cable, the stitches on the right side of the loom (when the loom is facing you) are held on the cable needle (without being worked) while you work on the stitches to the left. Depending on the direction you want on your cable, you will hold the cable needle either toward the center of the loom or toward the front of the loom. If the cable needle is held in front of the work, the cable will twist to the left. This is the left cross (LC), also known as front cross (FC). If the cable needle is held to the center of the loom (back of work), the cable will have a right twist. This is the right cross (RC), also known as the back cross (BC).

Left cross (LC)–2 stitches

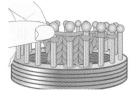 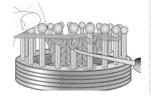

1 Take working yarn behind peg 1 (you are skipping peg 1).

2 Knit peg 2 and place stitch on cable needle and hold it to the center of the loom.

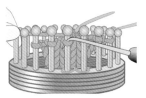 

3 Move stitch from peg 1 to peg 2 (leaving peg 1 empty).

4 Place stitch from cable needle on peg 1.

Purl cables with 2 stitches

Achieving left cross purl (LCP) and right cross purl (RCP) cables is easy.
LCP: Follow the left cross (LC) instructions except in step 2, purl instead of knit peg 2.
RCP: Follow the right cross (RC) instructions except in step 5, purl instead of knit peg 2.

5 Knit peg 2.

Right cross (RC)–2 stitches

 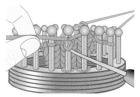

1 Place stitch from peg 1 on cable needle and hold to the center of the knitting loom.

2 Take working yarn in front of peg 2 and knit peg 2.

3 Move stitch from peg 2 to peg 1.

4 Place stitch from cable needle on peg 2.

 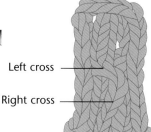

5 Knit peg 2.

Left cross —

Right cross —

Left cross (LC)–3 stitches

1 Take working yarn behind pegs 1 and 2 (you are skipping pegs 1 and 2).

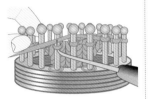

2 Knit peg 3. Place stitch from peg 3 onto cable needle.

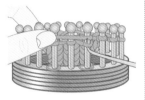

3 Knit peg 1 and peg 2. Move them over to pegs 2 and 3 as follows: stitch from peg 2 to peg 3, stitch from peg 1 to peg 2.

4 Place the stitch from cable needle on peg 3. Knit peg 3.

Right cross (RC)–3 stitches

1 Place stitch from peg 1 to cable needle and hold to center of knitting loom.

2 Knit peg 2 and peg 3.

3 Move the stitches from pegs 2 and 3 to pegs 1 and 2.

4 Place the stitch from cable needle on peg 3. Knit peg 3.

Left cross (LC)–4 stitches

1 Take working yarn behind pegs 1 and 2 (you are skipping pegs 1 and 2).
2 Knit peg 3 and 4. Place loops from pegs 3 and 4 on cable needle.
3 Knit pegs 1 and 2. Move them over as follows: stitch from peg 2 to peg 4; stitch from peg 1 to peg 3.
4 Take the stitches off the cable needle and place them on pegs 1 and 2.
5 Go to each of the stitches on pegs 1–4 and gently pull out any yarn slack so it tightens the cable.

Right cross (RC)–4 stitches

1 Remove stitches from pegs 1 and 2 and place them on cable needle.
2 Knit peg 3 and 4. Transfer stitches to pegs as follows: stitch from peg 3 to peg 1; stitch from peg 4 to peg 2.
3 Transfer the stitches from cable needle to emptied pegs 3 and 4. Knit these 2 stitches.
4 Go to each of the loops on pegs 1–4 and gently pull out any yarn slack so it tightens the cable.

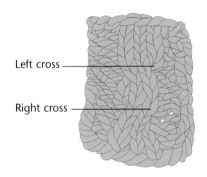

Left cross ———

Right cross ———

Purl cables with 3 stitches

To achieve left cross purl (LCP) and right cross purl (RCP) with 3 and 4 stitches, the crossing stitches are purled rather than knitted.
LCP: At step 2, purl instead of knit peg 3.
RCP: At step 4, purl instead of knit peg 3.

Increasing and decreasing stitches

Increase (inc)

This is adding extra stitches to the panel, thus making it wider. When increases happen within rows, it is recommended to only increase 2 stitches on a given row. Increases are used to shape items such as sweater sleeves, skirts, and items that fan out.

There are various ways to increase stitches on the loom, and all of them require you to move the stitches outward to the empty pegs to allow room, or an empty peg, for the new stitch. Below, you will find three methods. Familiarize yourself with all three of them.

Make 1 (m1)

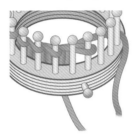

1 Move the last stitch to the next empty peg outward, leaving an empty peg between the last peg and the peg before last.

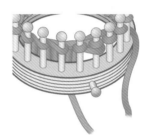

2 Make 1 (m1). Knit the stitches on the knitting loom: when you reach the empty peg, e-wrap it and continue knitting to the end of the row. Increasing in this manner will leave a small hole where the increase was created.

Lifted increase make 1

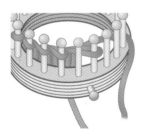

1 Move the last stitch to the next empty peg outward leaving an empty peg between the last peg and the peg before last.

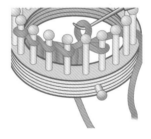

2 With the knitting tool reach for the running-ladder coming from the two stitches on either side below the empty peg. Twist the strand and place it on the empty peg (if you don't twist it, you will create a small hole). Knit your row as usual.

Yarn over (YO)

A yarn over is a decorative increase which creates a hole. It is often used in lace patterns. There are two ways to do this: e-wrap an empty peg or lay yarn in front of an empty peg.

Knitting into the front and back of a stitch (KFB)

1 Take yarn to the front of the peg where you would like the kfb. Work the peg as if to knit, however, do not remove the original loop off the peg, leave it at the base of the peg. The new loop is created and it is on the knitting tool.

2 Place this newly formed loop (the one on the knitting tool) on adjacent empty peg (or if no adjacent peg is empty, place it on a safety pin).

3 Work the peg again, this time, e-wrap the peg, work the peg by lifting the bottom loop up and off the peg.

Tip: Move the stitches first to create the empty pegs needed.

Decreases (dec)

Removing stitches from your panel will make the panel narrower. When decreases happen within rows, try to decrease 1 or 2 stitches in from either edge to keep the selvage neat. There are various ways to decrease on the knitting loom; all of them require you to move the stitches inward. Familiarize yourself with the methods below.

Knit 2 together (k2tog)

Knitting 2 together (k2tog) creates a right slanting decrease, and is best created at the beginning of a knit row.

Place stitch from peg 1 on peg 2, treat both loops on peg 2 as one loop, move these two loops over to peg 1, making sure to leave them in the order they are, treat both loops on the peg as one loop.

Slip, slip knit (SSK)

The left slanting decrease is the mirror image of a k2tog and is achieved by a slip, slip knit (ssk) at the end of a row.

Place stitch from peg 2 onto peg 1, treat both loops on peg 1 as one loop.

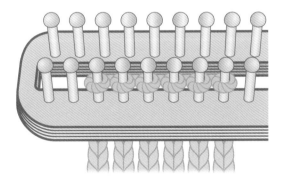

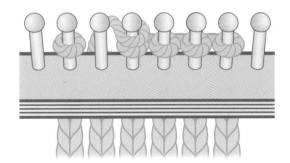

Working flat panels

Don't feel intimidated by the idea of creating a flat panel on a circular loom. It is a simple process that involves knitting on the knitting loom in a "C" shape.

From A to B and back again...

Knitting a flat panel on the knitting loom is not that different to circular knitting on the knitting loom. You can use the same cast-on methods, knit the same stitches, and use the same bind-off methods. However, there are a few things that differ.

Since you are not knitting in a circle around the knitting loom, you will have a starting point and an ending point. At both ends you will have a turning peg/stitch marking the beginning of a new row or the end of the last one.

When starting at point A, the peg at point A is your beginning peg. The peg at point B becomes your last peg and will also be your turning peg. When you finish a row by knitting the peg at point B, you turn and knit back to point A. Thus the pegs and point A and B alternate as turning pegs and beginning and ending pegs for the rows.

Beware of the selvage

Now you are no longer going round in circles, you will have edges to deal with. The edge stitches of a knitted panel are called edge or selvage stitches.

When knitting from a pattern look for instructions on how to treat the selvage stitches. One way is to wrap the turning pegs and knit them as above. Alternatively, you can slip stitch the first stitch on each row.

A slip stitch (sl st) is simply a stitch that is not knitted. You skip the peg and take the yarn to the next peg and knit it. Using a slip stitch at the beginning of each row creates a chainlike edge at both sides of the knitted item.

How do you decide which turning option to use? If you are going to be seaming two pieces together or adding a border, it is best to knit the edge stitches (always knit the first and last stitches). If you are looking for a more decorative edging, slip the first stitch of every row. However, slipping the stitch on each row will reduce the width of your knitted item by two stitches. If the pattern doesn't allow for this, you will have to add one stitch to either side of the pattern as you go along.

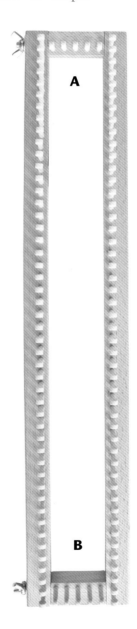

An introduction to double knitting

Working in double knit is so easy and fun with the use of knitting boards and looms. The knitter works across two rows of pegs, interlocking them into a single-layer fabric that is double-sided, with no back side. This means that the knots from tying on new skeins of yarn and changing colors are hidden between the two layers. There is no back side, so both sides of the knitting are the same and finished. This is great with designs using multiple colors and when wanting the fabric to be reversible. Afghans, shawls, and scarves can show off both sides of the knit.

When working in double knit, you can use thick yarn for a very thick knit; use fine yarn and you can create a beautiful open weave just like in single knit. The gauge is determined by the spacing between the two rows of pins or pegs. Double knit also has the advantage of not needing to be blocked. This is due to the double sides, so the edges do not roll or curl.

Double knitting stitches

Open rib stitch

Open rib is a nice chunky version of the traditional rib stitch. The two sides are different: the front is chunky and the back is a regular rib stitch. Work over an even number of stitches. To begin, cast on in stockinette. The working yarn will be coming from the left end of the front board.

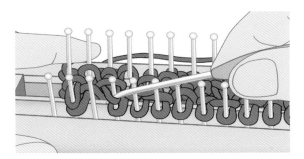

1 Move the loop at the left end of the back board to its right, placing it onto the second peg. Move the third loop onto the fourth peg. Continue across the back board in this manner, moving every other loop onto the peg to its right, so that every other peg on that side of the board has two loops and the ones between are empty. Leave the stitches on the front board as they are, one loop on each peg. The stitches are now ready to weave in the open rib stitch.

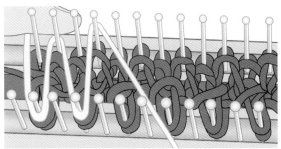

2 Starting at the left end and weaving the yarn back and forth around every other peg on each board as shown. You will work in stockinette and wrap the pins with 2 loops on the back board and every other on front board. Continue across the board. When you get to the end of the row, turn the board around and work back by wrapping the pins with 3 loops and working the pins on the opposite board in stockinette.

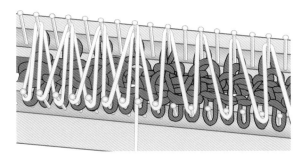

3 You will have pins with 4 wraps and adjacent pins that are empty; this is correct. The other side will have all pins wrapped.

4 To hook over the chunky side, lift the 2 bottom loops on each peg up and over, leaving the 2 top loops on each peg. Hook over other board by lifting one loop over another one. The empty pins will always remain empty. Repeat for all rows.

Crisscross stitch

This is a great stitch to use for an allover design or for an accent mixed with smooth stockinette. It has a lot of texture and contrast.

To begin, cast on using the method indicated in your project directions or stockinette. Position the board so the working yarn is coming from the left end of the front board. To work the crisscross stitch, first do a complete circular of weave pattern 1, then work a complete circular of weave pattern 2. Alternate the two weave patterns until the piece is the desired length.

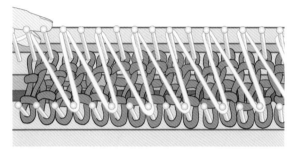

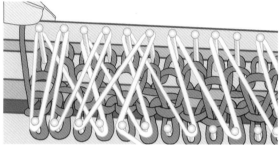

1 Starting at the left, wrap yarn from outside around first peg on back board, fourth peg on front, then third peg on back. Bring yarn forward to wrap peg 6 on front. Weave back and forth across the boards, skipping every other peg. Wrap last peg on the front and pass yarn back. Turn board around and knit stitch to the other end, wrap all the empty pegs: Peg 1 on the front, peg 2 on the back, peg 2 on the front, peg 4 on the back, peg 3 on the front. Continue as shown. Hook over all.

2 Weave Pattern 2.

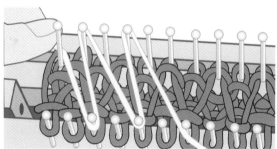

3 Wrap the yarn from the outside around peg 1 on the back board, around peg 3 on the front board, then around peg 2 on the back board. Bring the yarn forward to wrap peg 5 on the front board and back to wrap peg 4 on the back board.

4 Continue, weaving the yarn back and forth around every other peg on each board as shown. When you reach the end, wrap the last peg on the front board and pass the yarn straight back. Turn the board around. To return to the other end, wrap all the empty pegs as follows: Peg 1 on the front board, peg 3 on the back board, peg 2 on the front board. Continue, weaving the yarn back and forth around every other peg on each board as shown. To continue, hook over all pegs.

Joining yarns

When you least expect it, it happens—the yarn suddenly comes to an end or worse, breaks. It is time to attach a new yarn to the project.

To join a new yarn at the edge: Join the new yarn at the beginning of a row. If possible, join the yarn on an edge that will be within a seam.

Method 1: Leave a tail of about 5–6 in (12.5–15 cm) in length on the old skein and another tail the same length on the new skein. Hold the two yarns together and knit the first three stitches. Drop the old skein and continue knitting with the newly joined yarn.

Method 2: Leave a tail of about 5–6 in (12.5–15 cm) in length on the old skein and another tail the same length on the new skein. Tie a temporary knot with the two ends as close to the project as possible. Pick up the newly joined yarn and continue knitting. When the project is complete, go back and undo the knot. Weave in the ends in the opposite direction to close the gap formed by the change of yarns.

Stuck in the middle: Occasionally you will need to join yarn in the middle of a row. In this case, you can use method 2 above. Tie a temporary knot close to the project, making sure to leave a tail of about 5–6 in (12.5–15 cm) on both ends. Continue knitting with the new yarn. Make sure to undo the knot before weaving in the ends.

Finishing your work

Finishing off the cast-on edge

The anchor yarn is holding the first loops as "live" stitches. When the project is completed, the cast-on edge needs to be finished by crocheting. The following steps will show how to accomplish this essential step of the knitted garment. In order to finish the "live" stitches, you need to have a crochet hook that will work with the weight of yarn used.

Weaving the tail ends

When you have finished your project you still need to hide those unsightly yarn tail ends. Use a needle to hide them on the wrong side of the item.

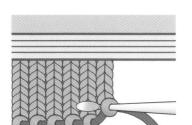

1 Insert crochet hook in the first stitch.

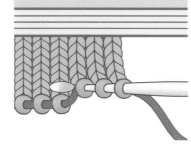

2 Insert the hook through the next two stitches.

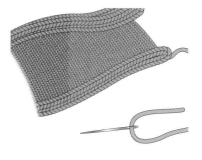

1 Locate the yarn tail end; thread it through the large eye of a tapestry needle.

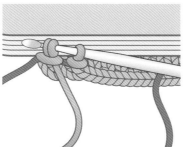

3 Pass the first stitch on the front of the hook through the middle stitch, and then pass it through the back stitch, leaving only 1 loop on the hook.

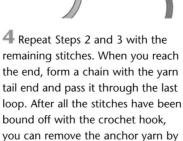

4 Repeat Steps 2 and 3 with the remaining stitches. When you reach the end, form a chain with the yarn tail end and pass it through the last loop. After all the stitches have been bound off with the crochet hook, you can remove the anchor yarn by pulling it out.

2 Working on the wrong side of the item weave the yarn tail end about 1 in (2.5 cm) in one direction by inserting the needle through the "bump" of each knit stitch. Go up/down one row weaving in for about 1 in (2.5 cm).

Steps 1–2 should create a "Z" with the tail end. Cut the remainder of the yarn as close to the knitted item as possible. Repeat this process with each yarn tail end you have in your knitted item.

Joining your knitting

Mattress stitch

1 Lay the pieces to be joined, right side up and side-by-side. Thread a tapestry needle with the tail end. Bring the yarn through to the front, in the middle of the first stitch on the first row of the seam. Take the needle through to the same position on the other piece, and bring it out in the middle of the edge stitch one row up.

2 Insert the needle back into the first piece of fabric, in the same place that the yarn last came out. Then bring the needle out in the middle of the stitch above. Repeat this making a zigzag seam from edge to edge for a few more rows. You can pull the thread firmly, and the stitches almost disappear. When the seam is finished, weave in the ends.

Seaming with the invisible stitch

This stitch creates an invisible seam in double knit. Insert a tapestry needle into the center of the edge and pick up the cross stitch in the center. Do exactly the same to the other piece. Pull the yarn snugly and the pieces will come together without the sewing yarn showing. Continue alternating the two sides until you have a completed seam.

Grafting

Also known as the Kitchener stitch, grafting allows you to join two panels of knitted fabric invisibly. The process is simple, although at first it may seem daunting. Just take it step-by-step and you will be on your way to invisible seams. In the case of socks, the toe area is grafted to the instep of the sock.

When you are preparing for grafting, you need to mount the stitches correctly on the needle. Correct position ensures proper grafting. Imagine the following: The knit stitch consists of two arms: a right and a left arm. While holding the needle on the left hand, the stitches should sit on the needle with the right arm toward the front of the work.

Preparation

1 Cut working yarn coming from the sock, leaving a 3 yd (3 m) tail.
2 Transfer half of the stitches from the loom onto one double-pointed knitting needle (in the example shown opposite, loops from pegs 1 through 12).
3 Transfer the remaining half of the stitches to a second double-pointed needle (in this example, loops from pegs 13 through 24).
4 Thread a tapestry needle with the 3 yd (3 m) tail.

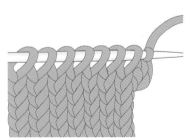

The stitches should sit as shown in the illustration above.

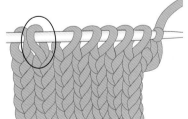

Incorrect mounting: note how the left arm toward the front of the needle faces left.

Working

For illustration purposes, a contrasting color yarn is used for the grafting row here.

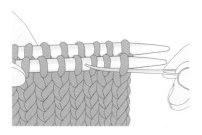

1 Hold knitting needles parallel to each other, wrong sides of the knitting together. Insert the tip of the tapestry needle through the first stitch on the front needle as if you were going to purl.

2 Insert yarn through the first stitch on the back needle as if to knit, pull the yarn through, but leave stitch on the knitting needle.

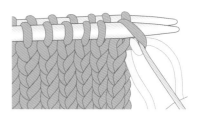

3 Insert the tip of the tapestry needle through the first stitch on the front needle as if you were going to knit, pull the yarn through the stitch, and slide that same stitch off the needle.

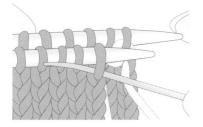

4 Insert the yarn needle through the next stitch on the front needle as if to purl, pull the yarn through, and leave the stitch on the needle.

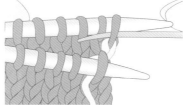

5 Bring the yarn to the side of the fabric (not over the needles) and insert the tapestry needle through the first stitch on the back needle as if to purl, bring the yarn through, and slide the stitch off the needle.

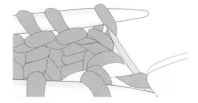

6 Insert the tapestry needle through the next stitch on the back needle as if to knit, pull the yarn through, and leave the stitch on the needle.

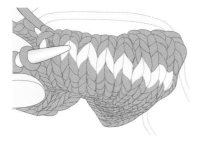

7 Repeat Steps 3–6 across the row of stitches until only one stitch remains. Insert the tapestry needle through that last stitch and weave in ends.

TIP

If there are any uneven stitches, use the tapestry needle to gently tug on the little legs of the adjacent stitch until the stitches look even throughout the row.

Blocking & embellishments

Blocking

Blocking is part of finishing any knitted item. It aids in evening out the stitches and in making a panel lie flat. Blocking is done after weaving in the ends and before seaming panels together.

To block, you will need rustproof pins, rustproof lace wires, a spray bottle or steam iron, towels/bedspread in a neutral color and a flat surface—a bed, or even a carpeted floor works well for this purpose.

Wet blocking: set the towels/bedspread on top of a flat surface, set the knitted item on top, spray it with cold water. Pin it along the edges—using the rustproof lace wires can facilitate the pinning process and provide you with straight edges. Let the item dry completely before removing the pins.

A note on wet blocking:
- Wet blocking over neutral colored towels/bedspread will ensure that there will be no color bleeding from the towels/bedspread to the knitted item.

Steam blocking: similar to wet blocking but instead of spraying the item with water, hover the steam iron a few inches above the knitted item and steam it. Pin it along the edges. Let the item dry completely before removing the pins.

A couple of notes on steaming:
- Steaming non-natural yarns may distort the yarn and even melt it. Only steam block items knitted with natural yarns.
- Steam block lightly over areas that need to retain their elasticity—such as ribbing.

A knitted item may need re-blocked after being worn and/or washed. Use the same method to re-block the item.

3-stitch I-cord

An I-cord is knitted with a knit stitch. Work on a loom in a clockwise direction (from right to left).

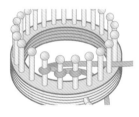

1 Cast on 3 pegs. With working yarn coming from the third peg, run the yarn behind the pegs to the first peg.

2 Bring yarn to the front of the loom and knit the 3 pegs.

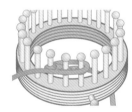

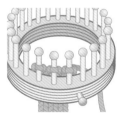

3 Knit the second peg, then the first, and the third last. Repeat until the cord measures the desired length.

4 Bind off by cutting the yarn, leaving a 4 in (10 cm) tail. Move the loop from second to first peg. Knit over. Move the loop on peg 1 to peg 2. Move the loop on peg 3 to peg 2. Knit over. With working yarn, e-wrap peg 2. Knit over. Pull the last loop off the peg and pull on the yarn tail end.

Tassels

Tassels are a decorative element made of strands of yarn tied at one end, typically seen at the corners of blankets.

 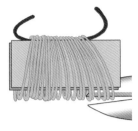  

1 You need two pieces of cardboard—the height of the cardboard corresponds to the length of the tassel. Sandwich a piece of yarn between the two pieces of cardboard. This is used later on to secure the top of the tassel.

2 To make the tassel, wind yarn around the cardboard; the more wraps around the cardboard, the bushier the tassel. Using the yarn sandwiched between the pieces of cardboard, secure the top of the tassel. Cut the strands at the bottom edge along the cardboard. Remove the cardboard pieces.

3 Wrap another length of yarn around the group of strands, about 1 in (2.5 cm) below the top— 5–10 wraps are recommended. Use the same color or a contrasting color for extra effect. Hide the ends of the yarn inside the tassel. Trim the tassel ends to look uniform.

4 Use the free ends at the top of the tassel to secure it to the knitted project.

Fringes

Fringes are a decorative element made out of strands of yarn. They are made of a set of tassels, but do not have a top yarn to secure them to the knitted fabric. Instead, they are drawn securely through the edge of the knitted fabric.

 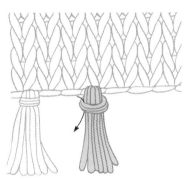

1 Follow Steps 1 and 2 from the Tassels instructions (above). Insert a crochet hook from front to back (or back to front) into the fabric's edge and pull the folded loop through the fabric.

2 Bring the ends through the loop and secure the tassel by tightening. Once all the fringe has been attached to the knitted fabric, trim the strands of yarn to the same length for a uniform look.

Working with color

Adding color to your knits is a great way to liven up your projects. Below are various ways that you can use color to spice up your knits.

Stripes

Creating stripes is the easiest way to add color to a project. Knitting stripes allows you to use as many colors as you wish without having to carry more than one color at a time within the row. Gather all your odd skeins and try wide stripes, narrow stripes or mixing wild colors and textured yarns. Your one-of-a-kind creation will have one main color (MC) with one (or more) contrasting colors (CC). When more than one contrasting color is used, the colors are designated by letters, such as A, B, C, D and so on.

Horizontal stripes

Knit a few rows with your main color. When it's time to change to a new color, join the new yarn at the beginning of a row. After you have your desired colors set up, you can carry the various yarns along the edge of the item if you are knitting thin stripes. If you are knitting wider stripes, cut the yarn at the end of a row and join yarns at the beginning of a row.

Vertical stripes

Creating thin vertical stripes is simple. You don't have to weave the yarns at the back of the work; the unused yarn can be carried behind the work. You will need yarn in two colors: a main color (MC) and a contrasting color (CC).

1 Pick up the MC and knit the stitches you desire in the main color; skip the ones you desire in contrasting color.
2 Go back to the beginning of the row, pick up the CC, and knit all the pegs skipped in Step 1.
3 Repeat Steps 1–2 throughout.

Jogless stripes
1 Knit the first round with MC: work normally.
2 Knit the second round with CC: skip the first stitch with yarn to the back of the stitch and work the rest of the stitches as indicated in the pattern.
3 Consecutive rounds are with CC: work normally.
4 Repeat above steps when creating more stripes.

Fair Isle

Fair Isle is a multicolored knitting technique where a row is worked with two colors in small repeating sections of pattern. Traditional Fair Isle knitting is worked completely in stockinette stitch, and the items are usually circular. The circular nature of the item helps to hide the floats (unused strands of yarn on the back of your work) created by the color changes within the row. When carrying the unused color, do not carry it over more than 5–7 stitches or 1–1½ in (2.5–4 cm). Fair Isle patterns are usually depicted in chart form and share some characteristics with regular knitting charts. Each square represents a stitch. The squares will either be colored in, or will have a color symbol and key. For circular knitting, you read the chart starting at the bottom, right side. Continue reading the next rounds starting at the right side. There are two methods.

Method 1
Pick up the main color at the beginning of a row, knit the required stitches, and then drop it at the end of the row. Pick up the contrasting color and knit all the required stitches with that color, then drop it.

Method 2
Carry both yarns with you in your dominant hand as you work the stitch pattern. When the pattern calls for the CC, drop the MC color, bring the CC above the MC working yarn, and knit as required. When the pattern calls for the MC, drop the CC and reach below for the MC color. Every time you change yarns, drop the one above and then reach for the other.

Weave the two colors around each other at the back of the work to prevent the holes.

To weave the yarns around each other: knit a few stitches with the MC, drop it and pick up the CC, wrap the CC around the MC, drop the CC, pick up the MC, and keep on knitting. Take both colors to the back of the work, and twist them together.

Fixing mistakes

So you have been happily knitting, then you look down and to your horror, you see a stitch dangling all by itself. What do you do? If it is one or two stitches, you can save the day.

On stockinette stitch side fabric

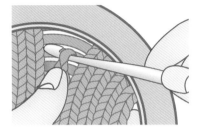  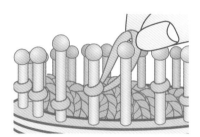

1 Insert the crochet hook from front to back through the stitch dropped.

2 Hook the first "ladder" or horizontal bar behind the stitch and pull it through the stitch to the front of the work.

3 Continue picking up the unraveled stitches by following Step 2. When all stitches have been picked up, place the last stitch back on the peg.

On purl side fabric

1 Insert crochet hook through the back side of the fabric (inside the circle of the loom or the wrong side of the fabric). Hook the dropped stitch.

2 Hook the unraveled strand behind the stitch and pull it through the stitch to the back of the fabric.

3 Continue picking up the unraveled stitches by following Step 2. When all stitches have been picked up, place the last stitch back on the peg.

Fixing stitches

If you accidentally knitted the wrong stitch on the row below, you have two options.

Option One: Work back the row, one stitch at a time, until you reach the stitch where the mistake is located. Fix the stitch and continue knitting.

Option Two: Drop the stitch on that column of stitches and fix the mistake.

If the problem is located a few rows back, it is best to unravel the knitting and undo the entire row with the mistake.

1 Use a piece of waste yarn or a circular needle to hold your stitches to act as a lifeline one row below the problem row.
2 Take the stitches off the pegs and unravel all the stitches until you reach the row with the lifeline that is your stitch holder.
3 Place the stitches back on the pegs. Make sure to position the stitches on the loom the correct way.

Short row shaping

This allows shaping a knitted panel without the aid of increasing stitches. It creates soft curves by knitting a row to a certain stitch in the row, then turning back and knitting in the other direction. It is a method commonly used in heels, blouse darts for the stomach or bust area, and in any other item where you want seamless curves.

Shaping with short-rows has one pitfall that you must be aware of. It is necessary to wrap the stitch after the turning point to avoid a hole between the turning stitch and the next stitch. The "wrap" eliminates the hole almost completely.

How to wrap and turn (W&T)

When knitting each wrapped peg, lift both the wrap and the stitch together, 2 over 1, as this will eliminate the wrap and fill the hole made with the short rows.

1 Knit or purl to the desired turning stitch. Take the stitch off the next peg and hold it with your knitting tool.

2 Wrap the peg by taking the yarn towards the inside of the loom and wrapping around the peg. The working yarn will end up to the front of the knitting loom.

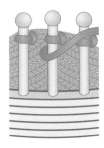

3 Place the stitch back on the peg. Take working yarn and knit or purl back across the row.

Reading charts

Charts are pictorial representations of stitch patterns, color patterns, or shaping patterns. Reading charts in loom knitting differs from reading a chart when needle knitting. In needle knitting (and when loom-knitting flat panels), the knitting is turned after every row, exposing the wrong and right side of the fabric every other row. In loom knitting, the right side of the fabric is always in front, so we follow the pictorial chart as it appears.

- Charts are visual and pictorial representations of the stitch pattern. A chart allows you to see the entire stitch pattern.

- Charts are numbered on both sides, even numbers on the right side, odd on the left.

- Start reading the chart on the bottom.

- Each square represents a stitch.

- Each horizontal row of squares represents a row.

- Stitch-pattern charts use symbols to represent stitches such as knit, purl, twists, yarn-overs, and any other stitch manipulation needed.

- Thick black lines represent the end of a pattern stitch repeat. The stitches after the black line are edge, or selvage, stitches.

- Charts for color knitting differ from stitch-pattern charts. In color-pattern charts each different color square represents the color needed on that particular stitch.

- For circular knitting, read the chart from bottom up from right to left.

- For flat knitting, read the chart from bottom up from right to left on odd rows, and from left to right on even rows.

- Remember: the right side of the knitted fabric is always facing the outside. Knit the stitches as they appear on the chart.

2	●		●	
	●		●	1

● **P Purl**

☐ **K Knit**

Chart reads:

For flat knitting:
Row 1: k1, p1, k1, p1.
Row 2: k1, p1, k1, p1.

For circular knitting:
Round 1: *k1, p1, rep from * to the end.
Round 2: *p1, k1, rep from * to the end.

A complete list of chart symbols and abbreviations used in this book is provided on the opposite page (we are using needle knitting standard abbreviations and symbols whenever possible).

Abbreviations

[ ]   work instructions in brackets as many times as directed

( )   work instructions in parentheses in the place directed

* *   repeat instructions between the asterisks as directed

*   repeat instructions following the single asterisk as directed

alt   alternate

approx   approximately

bc   back cross

beg   begin/beginning

bet or btw   between

BO   bind off

CA   color A

cab   cable

CB   color B

cbs   chunky braid stitch

cc   contrasting color

cm   centimeters

cn   cable needle

co   cast on

col   color

cont   continue

cr L   cross left

cr R   cross right

dbl   double

dec   decrease

diam   diameter

ds   double stitch

ew   e-wrap

foll   follow/following

fc   front cross

fs   flat stitch/knit stitch

ft   denotes foot or feet

g   denotes grams

g st   garter stitch

hs   half stitch

inc   increase

in(s)   denotes inches

K or k   knit

kbl   knit through back of loop. In looming this is created by e-wrap

kfb   knit into the front and back of the same stitch (see page 41)

k2tog   knit 2 together (see page 41)

KO   knitting over, lifting a loop up and off the peg

l   left

lc   left cross

lp(s)   loop(s)

Lt   left twist

m   meters

mb   make bobble

m1   make one—increase one stitch (see page 40)

MC   main color

mm   millimeters

mul   multiple

oz   ounces

P or p   purl

pfb   purl into the front and back of the same stitch

p2tog   purl 2 stitches together

pm   place marker

prev   previous

psso   pass slipped stitch over

rc   right cross

rem   remaining/remain

rep   repeat

rev st st   reverse stockinette stitch

rnd(s)   round(s)

rs   right side

rt   right twist

sc   single crochet

sel   selvage

sk   skip

skn   skein

skp   slip, knit, pass stitch over—creates a decrease

sl   slip

sl st   slip stitch

ss   single stitch

ssk   slip, slip, knit these two stitches together (see page 41)

ssp   slip, slip, purl these two stitches together (see page 41)

st(s)   stitch(es)

st st   stockinette stitch

tog   together

TW or tw   twist stitches for a mock cable

w&t   wrap and turn (see page 58)

wy   working yarn

yd(s)   denotes yards

yo   yarn over (see page 40)

PART TWO
Baby Blankets

Entrelac Baby Blanket

Add a splash of color with this lovely entrelac blanket. The woven look gives this design a deceptive intricate look, but you will fall in love with its ease.

MATERIALS

Knitting loom

Regular gauge, 80 peg. Sample made on the All-n-One

Yarn

Approx 800 yards of worsted weight yarn. Sample knit in Lion Brand Cotton Ease; shades: (A) Taupe, (B) Seaspray, (C) Almond, (D) Lime x 1 skein of each

Notions

Knitting tool, crochet hook size 3/D, 8 stitch holders (or scrap yarn), 10 stitch/peg markers

Gauge

8 sts x 13 = 2 in (5 cm) in blocked stockinette stitch

Size

25 x 28 in (64 x 70 cm)

Abbreviations

For a list of common abbreviations see page 61

k2tog Knit two stitches together
kfb Knit into the front and back of 1 stitch
m1 Make 1 stitch
p2tog Purl 2 stitches together
ssk Slip, slip, knit

INSTRUCTIONS

The pattern includes detailed instructions on creating the first base tier for the blanket (in brackets after the row instructions). "Turn" refers to turning and working in the opposite direction.

To pick up stitches, find the small spine of knit stitches going sideways. Insert crochet hook through one spine, hook working yarn, place loop you have created on first empty peg. *Insert crochet hook through next spine stitch, hook working yarn, place loop from the hook on next empty peg; rep from * until all necessary stitches have been picked up.

This blanket consists of segments each made up of 8 sts.

Using D, cast on 72 sts and prepare to work a flat panel.

BASE TRIANGLES

Each base triangle is worked over 8 sts. Each triangle is worked by working the 15 rows below. (After the first 15 rows, you will continue a new triangle next to the triangle just completed.) First triangle covers from peg 1-8, second from peg 9-16, third from peg 17-24, etc.

Tip

Place a stitch marker on pegs 1, 9, 17, 25, 33, 41, 49, 57, 65, 73 to aid you in working each triangle. Each time you start a new triangle, ignore the previous one and begin the new triangle at the peg with the stitch marker, which becomes your peg 1.

Using D work as follows:

Row 1: K1, turn. (K peg 1.)
Row 2 (and all even rows): K all sts on this section. (K peg 1.)
Row 3: Sl1, k1, turn. (Skip peg 1, k peg 2.)
Row 5: Sl1, k2, turn. (Skip peg 1, k pegs 1 and 2.)
Row 7: Sl1, k3, turn. (Skip peg 1, k pegs 1, 2, and 3.)
Row 9: S1, k4, turn. (Skip peg 1, k pegs 1, 2, 3, and 4.)
Row 11: Sl1, k5, turn. (Skip peg 1, k pegs 1, 2, 3, 4, and 5.)
Row 13: Sl1, k6, turn. (Skip peg 1, k pegs 1, 2, 3, 4, 5, and 6.)
Row 15: Sl1, k7. DO NOT TURN. Triangle completed. (Skip peg 1, k pegs 1, 2, 3, 4, 5, 6, and 7.)

Repeat from * to * to create the following triangles, until you reach the end of the row. These 15 rows form pattern. Rep Rows 1–15 to end of the row. Turn. Cut D, leaving a 6 in (15 cm) tail.

Join A for next Tier as follows:

TIER 1

Consists of Left and Right side triangles with squares in the center.

Left Side Triangle

Row 1: K1, turn. (K peg 1.)
Row 2: Kfb, turn. (K peg 1 as normal, e-wrap peg 1 again but do not remove original loop. Place new loop on knitting tool on empty peg to right of peg 1 (call this peg 0) turn.)

Row 3: K1, k2tog, turn. (K peg 0. Move loop from peg 1 to peg 2. K peg 2, treating both loops on peg as one loop. Peg 1 is empty.)

Row 4: K1, m1, k1, turn. (K peg 2. Reach for ladder between peg 1 and peg 0, twist ladder to create M1 and place on peg 1. K peg 1 and 0.)

Row 5: K2, k2tog, turn. (K peg 0 and peg 1. Move loop from peg 2 to peg 3, k peg 3, treating both loops as 1 loop.)

Row 6 (and every even row): K to last st, m1, k1. (Move loop from peg 1 to peg 2, leave peg 1 empty. K peg 3 and 2. Reach for the ladder between peg 1 and 0, twist the ladder to create the M1 and place it on peg 1. K from the peg that has the working yarn to peg 0.)

Row 7: K1, k2, k2tog, turn. (K peg 0, 1, 2, move loop from peg 3 to 4, k peg 4 treating both loops as 1.)

Row 9: K1, k3, k2tog, turn. (K peg 0, 1, 2, 3, move loop from peg 4 to 5, k peg 5 treating both loops as 1.)

Row 11: K1, k4, k2tog, turn. (K peg 0, 1, 2, 3, 4, move loop from peg 5 to 6, k peg 6 treating both loops as 1.)

Row 13: K1, k5, k2tog, turn. (K peg 0, 1, 2, 3, 4, 5, move loop from peg 6 to 7, k peg 7 treating both loops as 1.)

Row 15: K1, k6, p2tog, DO NOT TURN. (8 sts in left triangle). (K peg 0, 1, 2, 3, 4, 5, 6 move loop from peg 7 to 8, p peg 7 treating both loops as 1.)

Remove the 8 sts (from peg 8 to peg 0) to a stitch holder and place toward center of loom. The 8 empty pegs will be used in Row 1 of Middle Squares.

You will pick up stitches from the side of the base triangle below. Continue working the middle squares, working with same yarn as for the Left Side Triangle.

Middle Squares

Row 1: Pick up and k8 sts along the edge of next triangle (or square). Once you pick up the last stitch, place it on top of the next st of the next triangle (from the triangle/square below), k2tog, turn.

Row 2: K8, (start the k8 on the same peg that you did the k2tog in Row 1), turn.

Row 3, 5, 7, 9, 11, 13, 15: Sl1, k6, k2tog, turn.

Row 4, 6, 8, 10, 12, 14: k8 (Before knitting the row, move sts down to cover empty peg created). After Row 15, DO NOT TURN. Take these 8 sts and place on a stitch holder. Use the empty pegs for the sts picked up at Row 1. Repeat until all triangle sides from tier below have been picked up.

Right Side Triangle

At the corner of the second tier.

Row 1: Pick up and k8 sts along the edge of next triangle (square) from previous section.

Row 2 (and every even row): K to the end of this section, turn.

Row 3: Sl1, k5, k2tog, turn.

Row 5: Sl1, k4, k2tog, turn.

Row 7: Sl1, k3, k2tog, turn.

Row 9: Sl1, k2, k2tog, turn

Row 11: Sl1, k1, k2tog, turn.

Row 13: Sl1, k2tog, turn.

Row 15: K2tog. The remaining st becomes first st picked up for first square of next section. Cut A, leaving a 6 in (15 cm) tail.

Join B for next Tier as follows: All sts, except for the last one, are on stitch holders, leave them on holder until you need a stitch from each section.

TIER 2

Row 1: Pick up and k8 sts along the edge of the square/triangle. For the first square, the last st from the previous Tier counts as the first st picked up meaning you only need

to pick up 7 more sts. Once you have picked up all the sts, pick up st from next segment and place it on top of the last peg of this segment, work an ssk on this peg and turn.

Row 2: K8, turn.

Row 3: Sl1, k6, ssk, turn. (For SSK, pick up a st from tier closest to sts.)

Rows 4-15: Rep the last two rows a further 6 times. After Row 15, DO NOT TURN.

Rep Rows 1–15 until all segments have been worked to the end of the row. Cut B leaving a 6 in (15 cm) tail. Join C. Continue with C for next Tier as follows:

Rep Tiers 1 and 2 until desired length is reached, switching yarn colors, keeping the color pattern: A, B, C, D, then work Tier 1 again.

Work Final Tier Triangles in same color as base triangles.

FINAL TIER TRIANGLES

Row 1: Pick up and k8 sts along edge of next segment, the last st from previous Tier counts as the first picked up st. Once you have picked up all the sts, pick up the st from the next segment and place it on top of the last peg of this segment, work an ssk on this peg and turn.

Row 2 (and every even row): K to the end of section, turn.

Row 3: K2tog, k5, ssk, turn.

Row 5: K2tog, k4, ssk, turn.

Row 7: K2tog, k3, ssk, turn.

Row 9: K2tog, k2, ssk, turn.

Row 11: K2tog, k1, ssk, turn.

Row 13: K2tog, ssk, turn.

Row 15: Sl1, ssk, pass slipped st over, do not turn. The remaining st will count as first picked up st for next triangle. Work triangles to end of row/section. Fasten last stitch off.

Weave ends in. Block to measurements. If desired, work a single crochet border around edge.

Lace Baby Blanket

This beautiful baby blanket uses the softest wool, a gently draping textured design and is perfect for newborns or for naming ceremonies.

MATERIALS

Knitting loom

101 peg small gauge loom. Sample was knit using All-n-One knitting loom

Yarn

Approx 1020 yards of aran weight yarn. Sample shown in Lion Brand Yarn Pound of Love, white x 1 skein

Notions

Knitting tool

Gauge

11 sts x 15 rows = 2 in (5 cm) in stockinette stitch

Size

26 x 30 in (66 x 76 cm)

Abbreviations

For a list of common abbreviations see page 61

PATTERN NOTES

Before working odd rows, undo the e-wraps (yarn overs) on the pegs and place yarn ladder in front of peg (knit ladder as a normal stitch) Work first row from left to right.

INSTRUCTIONS

Cast on 101 pegs from right to left, prepare to work a flat panel.

Row 1 and all odd rows: Knit.
Row 2: P1, *yo, k3, sl1-k2tog-psso, k3, yo, k1; rep from * to end.
Row 4: P1, *k1, yo, k2, sl1-k2tog-psso, k2, yo, k1, p1; rep from * to end.
Rows 6: P1, *k9, p1; rep from * to end.
Row 8: P1, *k3, yo, sl1-k2tog-psso, yo, k3, p1; rep from * to end.
Repeat Rows 1–8: 17 more times.
Bind off with basic removal method. Weave in ends. Steam block lightly to 26 x 30 in (66 x 76 cm).

HOW TO WORK ROWS 2, 4, 6, 8

Breakdown shows repeat from * worked over 10 pegs. Number pegs 1 through 10 from right to left.
Row 2: P1, *yo, k3, sl1-k2tog-psso, k3, yo, p1; rep from *.
Move loops from peg 5 to 6 (peg 6 has 2 loops on it, for k2tog); peg 4 to 5; peg 3 to 4; peg 2 to 3; peg 1 to 2. Peg 1 is empty. E-wrap peg 1; k pegs 2, 3, 4; skip peg 5 with working yarn behind peg; k peg 6 (treat both loops as one); move loop from 6 to 5; on peg 5, lift off the bottom loop (KO) on peg 5 (for

psso); move loops from peg 7 to 6; peg 8 to 7; peg 9 to 8; k pegs 6, 7, 8; e-wrap peg 9; p peg 10.

Row 4: P1, *k1, yo, k2, sl1-k2tog-psso, k2, yo, k1, p1; rep from *.
Move loops from peg 5 to 6 (peg 6 has 2 loops for k2tog); peg 4 to 5; peg 3 to 4; peg 2 to 3. K peg 1; e-wrap peg 2; k pegs 3 and 4; skip peg 5 with working yarn behind it; k peg 6 (treat both loops as one, for k2tog); move loop from peg 6 to 5; k bottom loop on peg 5 (to create psso); move loops from peg 7 to 6, peg 8 to 7; k pegs 6 and 7; e-wrap peg 8. k peg 9; p peg 10.

Row 6: p1, *k2, yo, k1, sl1-k2tog-psso, k1, yo, k2, p1.
Move loops from peg 5 to 6; peg 4 to 5; peg 3 to 4. K pegs 1 and 2; e-wrap peg 3; k peg 4; skip peg 5 with working yarn behind it (for sl1); k peg 6 (treat both loops as one for k2tog); move loop from peg 6 to peg 5; k bottom loop on peg 5 (this creates the psso); move loop from 7 to 6; k peg 6; e-wrap peg 7; k pegs 8 and 9; p peg 10.

Row 8: P1, *k3, yo, sl1-k2tog-psso, yo, k3, p1; rep from *.
Move loops from peg 5 to 6; peg 4 to 5; k pegs 1, 2, 3; e-wrap peg 4; skip peg 5 with working yarn behind it (for sl1); k peg 6 (treat both loops as 1 for k2tog); move loop from 6 to 5; k bottom loop on peg 5 (to create psso); e-wrap peg 6; k pegs 7, 8, 9; p peg 10.

Cable Baby Blanket

Garter stitch borders surround the sumptuous narrow cables which accent the body of this cozy blanket.

MATERIALS

Knitting loom

125-peg small-gauge knitting loom. Martha Stewart Knitting Loom, configured at 125 small blue pegs was used in sample

Yarn

Approx 1200 yards of worsted weight yarn. Sample shown in KnitPicks Chroma, Natural x 6 skeins

Notions

Tapestry needle

Gauge

18 sts x 30 rows = 4 in (10 cm) in stitch pattern

Size

Approximately 36 x 36 in (91 x 91 cm)

Abbreviations

For a list of common abbreviations see page 61

PATTERN NOTES

Charts for the cables can be found on page 73.

INSTRUCTIONS

CO 125 sts and prepare to work a flat panel.
Row 1: *P2, 4-st LC, p2, p5; rep from *, to last 8 sts p2, 4-st RC, p2
Rows 2–6: *P2, k4, p2, k5; rep from *, end p2, k4, p2

Rep rows 1–6 until item measures 23 in (58 cm) from cast-on edge.
BO
Weave in ends. Block lightly.

Border

CO 15 sts
Row 1: K
Row 2: P
Rep rows 1 and 2 until piece measures 118 in (325 cm) (or length needed to go around the blanket).

Bind off.

Weave in ends. Block lightly.

FINISHING

Using mattress stitch, seam the border to the blanket.

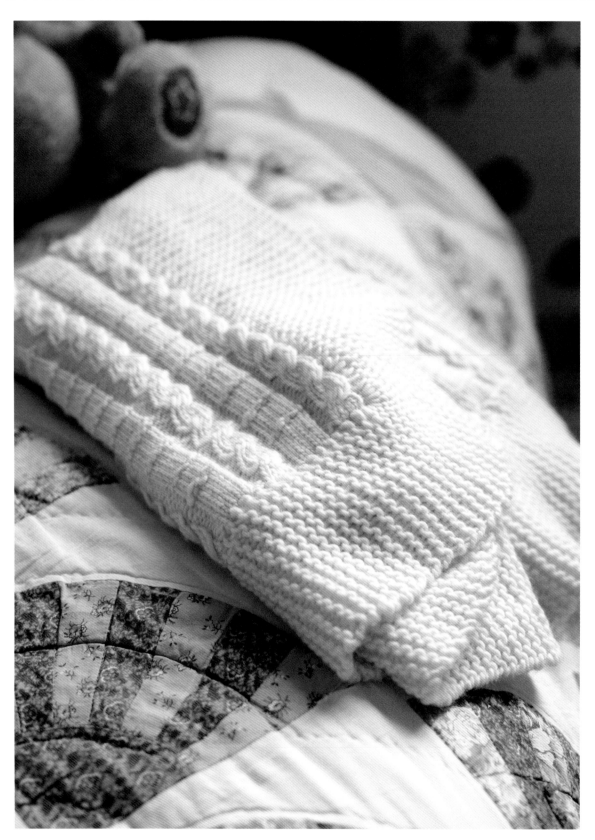

CABLECHART

	13	12	11	10	9	8	7	6	5	4	3	2	1	
						●	●					●	●	5
4						●	●					●	●	
						●	●					●	●	3
2						●	●					●	●	
	●	●	●	●	●	●	●	⟋⟍		⟍⟋		●	●	1

LEGEND

purl
purl stitch

c2 over 2 right
RS: sl2 to CN, hold in front. k2,k2 from CN

knit
knit stitch

Alphabet Baby Blanket

Knit a cozy baby blanket for baby with all the letters of the alphabet. Work it in a solid color or in a striped sequence.

MATERIALS

Knitting loom

Regular gauge knitting loom with 105 pegs. Sample was knit using All-n-One knitting loom

Yarn

Approx 900 yards of worsted weight yarn. Sample was worked using Martha Stewart Craft Extra Soft Wool Blend yarn in Lemon Chiffon x 6 skeins

Notions

knitting tool, row counter, crochet hook US size J/10 (6 mm)

Gauge

20 sts x 30 rows = 4 in (10cm) square over stockinette stitch

Size

26 x 30 in (66 x 76 cm)

Abbreviations

For a list of common abbreviations see page 61

PATTERN NOTES

The blanket is worked all in one piece. You will follow the layout provided to knit the blanket. Read the layout from Right to Left, Bottom to Top. You will be working 5 different squares over 38 rows. At the end of 38 rows, you will switch to the next set of letters.

INSTRUCTIONS

Cast on 105 sts, prepare to work a flat panel.

Row 1 should be from a R to L direction.

Row 1: Over the first 21 sts, work the Heart Square, work the Z square over the next 21 sts, work the Y square over the next 21 sts, work the X square over the next 21 sts, work the Heart Square over the last 21 sts.

Blanket layout

♡	A	B	C	♡
D	E	F	G	H
I	J	K	L	M
N	O	P	Q	R
S	T	U	V	W
♡	X	Y	Z	♡

LEGEND

	k on RS, p on WS
●	p on RS, k on WS

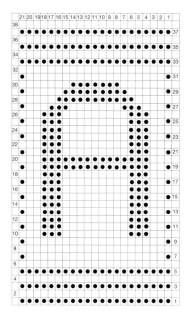

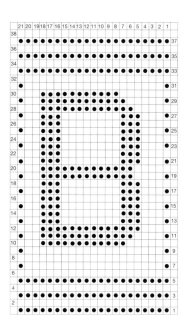

Row 2: Over the first 21 sts, work the Heart Square, work the X square over the next 21 sts, work the Y square over the next 21 sts, work the A square over the next 21 sts, work the Heart Square over the last 21 sts.

Next 38 rows:
Row 1: Over the first 21 sts, work the W square, work the V square over the next 21 sts, work the U square over the next 21 sts, work the T square over the next 21 sts, work the S square over the last 21 sts.
Row 2: Over the first 21 sts, work the S Square, work the T square over the next 21 sts, work the U square over the next 21 sts, work the V square over the next 21 sts, work the W over the last 21 sts.

Rep last two rows until you reach row 38.

Next 38 rows:
Row 1: Over the first 21 sts, work the R square, work the Q square over the next 21 sts, work the P square over the next 21 sts, work the O square over the next 21 sts, work the N square over the last 21 sts.
Row 2: Over the first 21 sts, work the N Square, work the O square over the next 21 sts, work the P square over the next 21 sts, work the Q square over the next 21 sts, work the R over the last 21 sts.

Rep last two rows until you reach row 38.

Next 38 rows:
Row 1: Over the first 21 sts, work the M square, work the L square over the next 21 sts, work the K square over the next 21 sts, work the J square over the next 21 sts, work the I square over the last 21 sts.
Row 2: Over the first 21 sts, work the I Square, work the J square over the next 21 sts, work the K square over the next 21 sts, work the L

square over the next 21 sts, work the M over the last 21 sts.
Rep last two rows until you reach row 38.

Row 1: Over the first 21 sts, work the H square, work the G square over the next 21 sts, work the F square over the next 21 sts, work the E square over the next 21 sts, work the D square over the last 21 sts.

Row 2: Over the first 21 sts, work the D Square, work the E square over the next 21 sts, work the F square over the next 21 sts, work the G square over the next 21 sts, work the H over the last 21 sts.

Rep last two rows until you reach row 38.

Last 38 rows:
Row 1: Over the first 21 sts, work the Heart Square, work the C square over the next 21 sts, work the B square over the next 21 sts, work the A square over the next 21 sts,

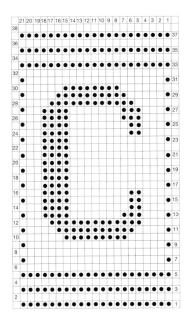

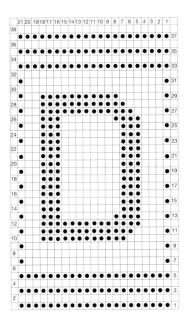

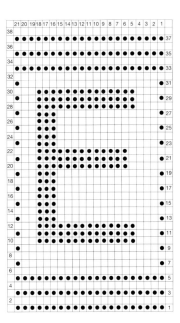

work the Heart Square over the last 21 sts.

Row 2: Over the first 21 sts, work the Heart Square, work the A square over the next 21 sts, work the B square over the next 21 sts, work the C square over the next 21 sts, work the Heart Square over the last 21 sts.

Rep last two rows until you reach row 38.

Bind off loosely. Weave ends in. Block lightly.

FINISHING

Using single crochet, work a single crochet round around the perimeter of the blanket.

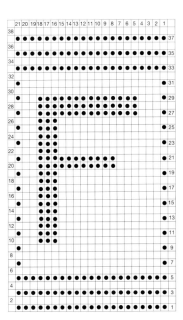

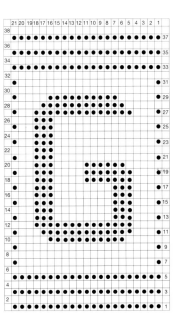

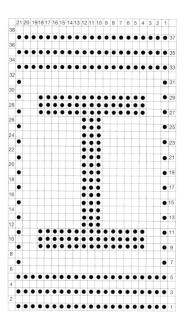

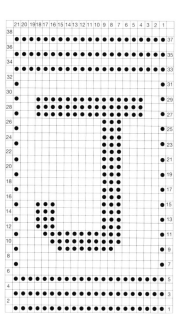

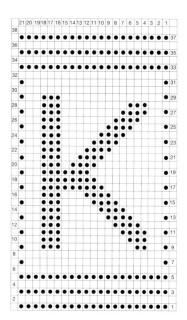

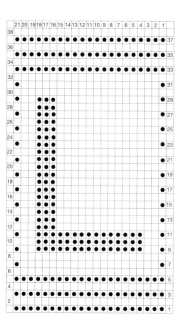

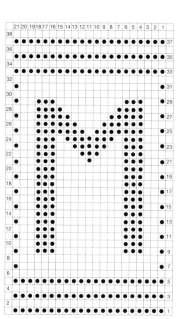

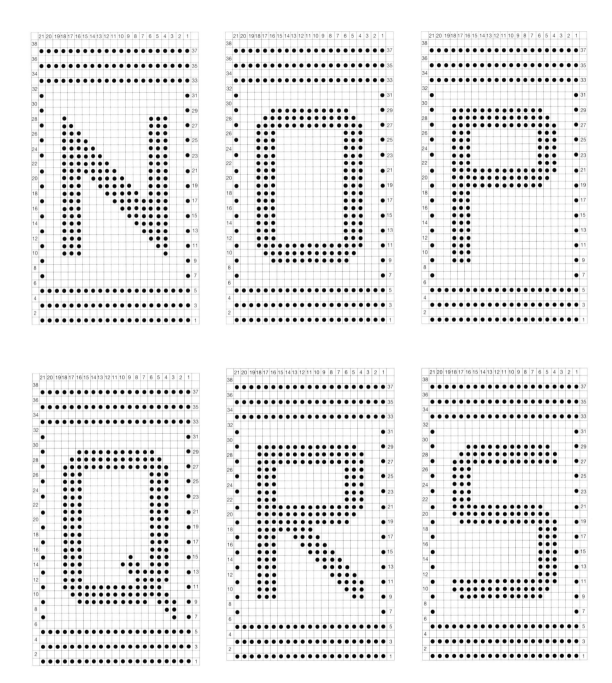

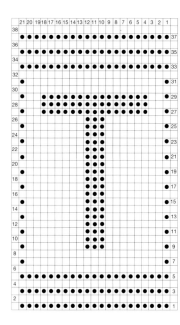
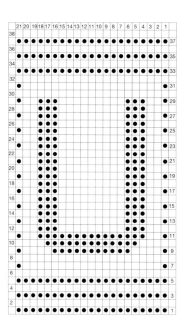
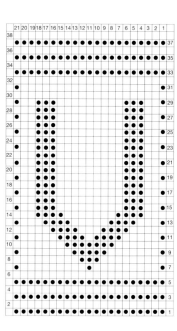

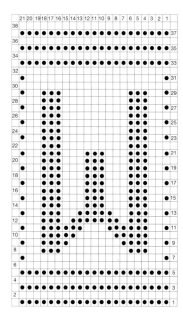
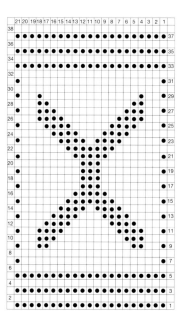
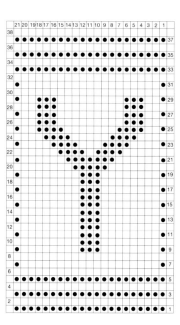

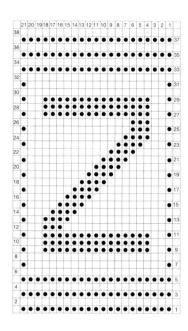

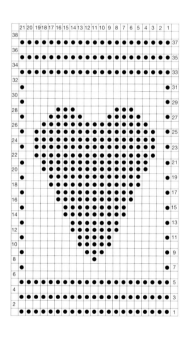

Stroller Stripes Blanket

Keep baby warm while riding on the stroller with this lovely striped blanket. On warmer days it will double as a playmat when you're enjoying a playdate in the park.

MATERIALS

Knitting loom

Regular gauge, 126 peg. Sample made on the Super Afghan Loom

Yarn

Approx 900 yards of worsted weight yarn. Shown in Lion Brand Cotton Ease; (MC) Turquoise x 3 skeins, (CC) Snow x 2 skeins

Notions

Knitting tool, tapestry needle

Gauge

9 sts = 2 in (5 cm) over stockinette stitch

Size

28 x 32 in (70 x 80 cm)

Abbreviations

For a list of common abbreviations see page 61

INSTRUCTIONS

With MC, cast on 126 sts and prepare to work a flat panel.

Row 1: Knit.
Row 2: Purl.
Rows 3–4: As rows 1–2.
Row 5: Knit.
Join CC.
Rows 6 and 8: Using MC, p4, drop MC, pick up CC, k to last 4 pegs, drop CC, pick up MC, p4.
Rows 7 and 9: Using MC, k4, drop MC, pick up CC, p to last 4 pegs, drop CC, pick up MC, k4.
Rows 10, 12 and 14: Using MC, p4, k to last 4 sts, p4.
Rows 11, 13 and 15: Using MC, Knit.

Rep rows 6–15, until piece measures 30 in (76 cm).

Using MC
Next row: Purl.
Next row: Knit.
Next row: Purl.
Next row: Knit.
Next row: Purl.

FINISHING

Bind off loosely. Weave in ends.

Block.

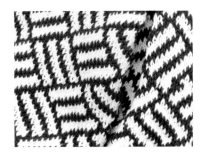

Colorwork Car Seat Blanket

Keep baby warm while traveling with this colorful car seat blanket. The contrast colors will keep baby entertained while the fabric backing covers the yarn floats protecting little fingers from getting caught.

MATERIALS

Knitting loom

Regular gauge, 108 peg. Sample made on the All-n-One

Yarn

Approx 1100 yards of worsted weight yarn. Sample shown in Debbie Bliss Cashmerino Aran; (MC) Mallard x 6 skeins; (CC) Ecru x 6 skeins

Notions

Knitting tool, tapestry needle

Other

Piece of backing fabric, 26 x 62 in (66 x 158 cm)

Gauge

9 sts x 18 rows = 2 in (5 cm) over stockinette stitch

Size

24 x 60 in (60 x 150 cm)

Abbreviations

For a list of common abbreviations see page 61

PATTERN NOTES

When knitting colorwork patterns, it is important to carry unused yarn loosely at the back of work. If the yarn is traveling more than ½ in (1.25 cm), weave the yarns along as you work the row to avoid long floats at back of work.

It is recommended to wash, dry, and iron the fabric prior to sewing it to the knitted backing of the blanket.

INSTRUCTIONS

Using MC, crochet cast on 108 sts using the crochet cast on method. Work in stockinette stitch, using knit stitch on odd-numbered rows and purl for even-numbered rows.

Row 1: Work Row 1 of chart, repeating the pattern 6 times across the row.
Row 2: Work Row 2 of chart, repeating the pattern 6 times across the row.

These 2 rows set the pattern.

Work in pattern and stockinette stitch as set through rows 1–18 of chart a total of 15 times, until the panel measures approx 60 in (150 cm) from cast-on edge.

Bind off using the basic bind off method. Weave ends in.
Block.

Border

Using CC, make an I-cord 168 in (428 cm) long. Seam I-cord to the edge of the blanket.

FINISHING

Either by sewing machine or by hand: using a 1in (2.5 cm) seam allowance, pin the fabric in place to wrong side of blanket, sew the backing in place.

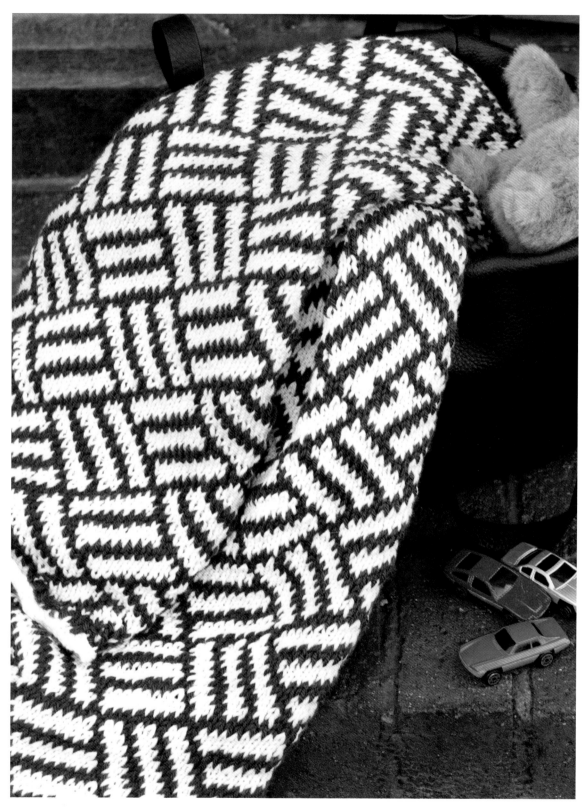

CHART

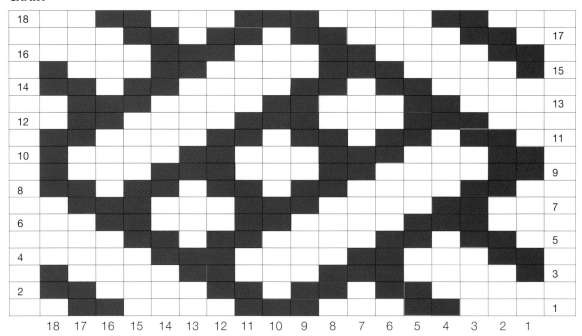

LEGEND

MC (Mallard)

CC (Ecru)

Gentle Waves Baby Blanket

A lightweight, easy care blanket for baby. Gentle wave designs at both ends makes this an easy, double knit blanket with a little fun mixed in. The body of the afghan is worked in stockinette stitch with some colorful accents in a Figure-8 stitch pattern. You'll have lots of fun making this one.

MATERIALS

Knitting loom

28 inch Knitting Board + peg extenders by Authentic Knitting Board; blanket requires 64 double stitches, 1 cm spacer

Yarn

Worsted weight yarn appropriate yarn for baby items. Sample shown in the following 2 yarns: (MC) 990 yards of Martha Stewart Extra Soft Blend Baby Worsted; shade: Winter Sky Blue x 6 skeins, (CC) 109 yards of Premier Serenity Chunky; shade: Aqua Glass x 1 skein

Notions

Knitting hook, crochet hook US F/5 (3.75 mm) or G/6 (4 mm)

Gauge

10 sts x 16 rows = 4 in (10 cm)

Size

20 x 40 in (50 x 100 cm)

Abbreviations

For a list of common abbreviations see page 61

PATTERN NOTES

Stockinette stitch: Peg #1 back to peg #2 front board. Continue wrapping every other peg to end of loom. Turn loom around and complete the row by weaving return, covering all pegs. Hook over. Figure 8: Wrap yarn around both pegs of one stitch as you would draw a number eight. They will be twisted in center between pegs. You will complete the row with only one pass down the loom.

INSTRUCTIONS

Work each of the scallops with a separate yarn of main color. Divide 2 skeins so that you have 4 partial balls. The first ball should be a full skein as you will continue with this one after the scallops.

With MC cast on in Figure 8 for each section. Lay anchor yarn over each section separately after cast on is complete.
Working left to right, using full skein, start on peg #5 with a loop knot. Cast on 3 sts.

With 2nd ball of yarn (partial), cast on with loop knot starting at peg #18. Work 3 sts.

With 3rd ball of yarn (partial), cast on starting at peg #31 and work 3 sts.

With 4th ball of yarn (partial), cast on starting at peg #44 and work 3 sts.

Cast on last scallop starting on peg #57 with partial skein, and work 3 sts.

You now have 5 sections, each with its own ball of yarn and 3 cast-on sts.

Increase row: Increase with a new st in front and at end of the 3 sts. Work peg to left of cast on st in Figure 8 once, and continue to end of section in stockinette stitch. At end, add the new stitch with 2 wraps of Figure 8 on peg to right of cast on stitches. Continue with stockinette stitch back to start of section. You now have 2 wraps on each of 5 pegs. Work the sts. Do this to all sections with connected yarns.

Row 2: Work this increase row so that there are now 5 sts in each section.

Row 3: Repeat the increases for each section so that you will complete the row with 7 sts in each section.

Row 4: You will have 9 sts in each section.

Row 5: You will have 11 sts in each section.

Row 6: You will have 13 stitches in each section (except the first at beginning of board) and all pegs should be covered.

Do not judge your shape of the scallops at this time as they will fan out and look lacey once you have more knitting complete.

You will now work with only the strand of yarn at beginning of the board. Cut all the rest of the attached yarns leaving approx 3–4 in (7.5–10 cm) tails. Use the crochet hook to bring each yarn tail over to next section, between the rows of pegs, and loosely tie a knot with a strand of yarn in next section, leaving the yarn tail laying between the rows of pegs.

Work 5 rows in stockinette stitch across all pegs.

Row 12: Work one row of main color in Figure 8 st. Tie CC to the 2nd stitch on next row. Leave the main yarn attached.

Row 13: Work with CC in figure 8 pattern. Cut and tie CC.

Rows 14 and 15: Work in MC in Figure 8 stitch.

Work stockinette stitch in MC for 10 in (25 cm).

Repeat rows 12 through 15 then work stockinette stitch in MC for 10 in (25 cm) twice more.

Work 2 rows in Figure 8 with MC. Work 1 row of CC in Figure 8 stitch. Cut CC and knot.
Work 1 row in Figure 8 with MC. Work 5 rows in stockinette stitch with MC.

Attach a MC yarn (partial) ball to each of sts #14, #27, #40, #53. Remember each section must have a separate ball of yarn attached. Work 1 row in each section with attached yarn ball in stockinette stitch.

Decrease rows:
Work the dec stitch at first and last stitch of each section so that each section is reduced by 2 sts. Do this by moving first loop over onto 2nd peg.
Move the last loop onto the adjacent peg to left. You now have 2 loops on the first and last peg of each section.
Weave the yarn onto the existing pegs and hook over being sure to

pick up both loops on the first and last pegs.

Repeat the dec rows until each section has only 5 loops remaining. The last section will only have 4 remaining. Work last dec row in Figure 8. Bind off very loosely and knot the yarn in each section.

FINISHING
Remove the afghan from loom. Tuck all yarn tails into the knit with crochet hook.
Finish the afghan by loosely binding off at the beginning stitches at the anchor yarns. Tuck in all yarn tails. Weave in ends.

Block.

PART THREE

Throws & Afghans

Ripple Lace Throw

Cozy up next to a fireplace with your favorite book and this luxurious throw.

MATERIALS

Knitting loom

Regular gauge, 198 peg. Sample made on the Super Afghan Loom

Yarn

Approx 1900 yards of worsted weight yarn. Sample shown in Cascade 220; shade: Smoke Heather x 9 skeins

Notions

Knitting tool, tapestry needle

Gauge

9 sts x 10 rows = 2 in (5cm) over stockinette stitch

Size

44 x 56 in (112 x 142 cm)

Abbreviations

For a list of common abbreviations see page 61

STITCH PATTERN
Ripple stitch

Row 1: *[K2tog] 3 times, [k1, yo] 6 times, [k2tog] 3 times; rep from * to end.

Row 2: Purl.

Row 3: Knit.

Row 4: Knit.

These 4 rows set pattern. Rep Rows 1–4 throughout.

Step-by-step breakdown of Row 1 worked over 18 sts:
Number the pegs as follows from right to left: 18, 17, 16, 15, 14, 13, 12, 11, 10, 9, 8, 7, 6, 5, 4, 3, 2, 1.

Step 1: Move sts from peg 1 to peg 2; from peg 3 to peg 4; from peg 5 to peg 6.

Step 2: Knit peg 2 (treat both loops on peg as one loop). Move loop from peg 2 to peg 1.

Step 3: Knit peg 4 (treat both loops on peg as one loop). Move loop from peg 4 to peg 2.

Step 4: Knit peg 6 (treat both loops on peg as one loop). Move loop from peg 6 to peg 3. Tug gently on working yarn to pull any yarn slack. Pegs 4, 5, 6 are empty.

Step 5: Knit peg 7 and move loop to empty peg 4. YO on peg 5.

Step 6: Knit peg 8 and move loop to empty peg 6. YO on peg 7.

Step 7: Knit peg 8 and move loop to empty peg 8. YO on peg 9.

Step 8: Move sts from peg 17 to peg 18; from peg 15 to 16; from peg 13 to 14. Move the two loops that are on peg 16 to peg 17; move the two loops that are on peg 16 to peg 17. Pegs 15, 14, 13 are empty.

Step 9: Move st from peg 12 to peg 14.

Step 10: Move st from peg 11 to peg 12.

Step 11: Knit peg 10. YO on peg 11.

Step 12: Knit peg 12. YO on peg 13.

Step 13: Knit peg 14. YO on peg 15.

Step 14: Knit pegs 16, 17, 18 (treat both loops on each peg as one loop).

INSTRUCTIONS
Cast on 198 sts and prepare to work a flat panel.

Commence Ripple Stitch pattern.

Repeat Rows 1–4 of Ripple Stitch pattern until panel measures approx 55 in (140 cm) from cast-on edge.

Bind off loosely. Weave ends in.

Block.

Chevron Throw

A gorgeous and colorful chevron blanket worked in garter stitch and four contrasting colors. Use different colors to create a unique throw for everyone in your family.

MATERIALS

Knitting loom

Regular gauge, 198 peg. Sample made on the Super Afghan Loom

Yarn

Approx 1600 yards of worsted weight yarn. Sample shown in Lion Brand Cotton Ease; shades: (A) Terracotta, (B) Cactus, (C) Snow, (D) Seaspray x 3 skeins of each

Notions

Knitting tool, tapestry needle, crochet hook US size J (6 mm)

Gauge

9 sts x 18 rows = 2 in (5 cm) over stockinette stitch

Size

44 x 56 in (112 x 142 cm)

Abbreviations

For a list of common abbreviations see page 61
k2tog Knit 2 stitches together
kfb Knit into the front and back of 1 stitch
ssk slip, slip, knit

STITCH PATTERNS

Chevron Stitch (worked over 16 rows)
Rows 1 and 3: With A, *k2tog, k4, kfb, k1, kfb, k4, ssk; rep from * to end.
Rows 2 and 4: Purl.
Rows 5 and 7: With B, *k2tog, k4, kfb, k1, kfb, k4, ssk; rep from * to end.
Rows 6 and 8: Purl.
Rows 9 and 11: With C, *k2tog, k4, kfb, k1, kfb, k4, ssk; rep from * to end.
Rows 10 and 12: Purl.
Rows 13 and 15: With D, *k2tog, k4, kfb, k1, kfb, k4, ssk; rep from * to end.
Rows 14 and 16: Purl.
These 16 rows form the Chevron Pattern and are repeated throughout.

Tip: Move the stitches first to create the empty pegs needed.

STITCH BREAKDOWN

Over 15 pegs, the breakdown is as follows, row is worked from right to left (clockwise):
Move stitch from peg 1 to 2.
Move stitch from peg 3 to 2.
Move stitch from peg 4 to 3.
Move stitch from peg 5 to 4.
Move stitch from peg 6 to 5.
Peg 6 is empty.
Peg 7 has a stitch, leave it as is.
Peg 8 has a stitch, leave it as is.
Lift loop from peg 15 and hold it.
Move stitch from peg 14 and place it on peg 15.

Place loop that you are holding from * back on peg 15.
Move stitch from peg 13 to 14.
Move stitch from peg 12 to 13.
Move stitch from peg 11 to 12.
Move stitch from peg 10 to 11.
Move stitch from peg 9 to 10.
Work the row as instructed.

INSTRUCTIONS

With A, cast on 195 sts and prepare to work a flat panel.
Commence Chevron pattern changing color every 4 rows.

TIP: When changing color, cut yarn leaving a 6 in (15 cm) tail and weave ends in as you work along the row.

Rep Rows 1–16 of Chevron Stitch pattern until panel measures approx 55 in (140 cm) from cast-on edge.

Bind off loosely with basic bind off method.

Weave ends in.

Block blanket.

FINISHING

Using crochet hook, crochet a single crochet border around blanket to stabilize it.

Garter Stitch Afghan

The garter stitch provides a perfect stitch that will produce a noncurling afghan while the yarn makes it soft and cuddly.

MATERIALS

Knitting loom

Regular gauge 198 peg. Sample made on the Super Afghan Loom

Yarn

Approx 2800 yards of worsted weight yarn. Sample knit in Lion Brand Homespun; shade: Apple Green x 16 skeins

Notions

Knitting tool, tapestry needle

Gauge

8 sts x 16 rows = 2 in (5 cm) over stockinette stitch

Size

52 x 56 in (132 x 142 cm)

Abbreviations

For a list of common abbreviations see page 61
ss   Single stitch/e-wrap stitch (see page 36)

INSTRUCTIONS

Cast on 198 sts and prepare to work a flat panel.

Row 1: SS.
Row 2: Purl.

Rep these two rows until panel measures 55 in (140 cm) from cast-on edge.

Bind off loosely. Weave ends in.

Block.

Twist of Lime Cable Throw

A fun and chunky double knit afghan for your sofa or to snuggle under as a lap blanket. Chunky ribs and a basic cable make this a fun one-day project.

MATERIALS

Knitting loom

28 inch Knitting Board + peg extenders by Authentic Knitting Board; blanket requires 64 double stitches, 1cm spacer

Yarn

Approx 1200 yards of soft chunky yarn. Sample shown in KnitPicks Cadena Yarn; shade: Mochi Green x 11 skeins + 1 extra for the optional fringe

Notions

Knitting hook, crochet hook, peg markers x 11, length of contrasting yarn for anchor yarn

Gauge

10 sts x 16 rows = 4 in (10 cm) over stockinette stitch

Size

26 x 40 in (66 x 100 cm)

Abbreviations

For a list of common abbreviations see page 61

STITCH PATTERNS

Open rib: On one side of loom, shift the 2nd loop to peg 1 so that peg 1 has 2 loops and peg 2 is empty. Shift loop on peg 4 over to peg 3 so that peg 3 has 2 loops and peg 4 is empty. Continue across the loom by shifting every other loop to the adjacent peg. Once complete, you will have 2 loops on every other peg with all others empty. The other board will have 1 loop on all pegs. When you weave, always wrap the peg with the loops so that you have 4 loops on these pegs and the adjacent ones remain empty. When you hook over, lift 2 loops (lower), leaving 2 loops on the pegs.

Cable twist: Start with double peg 1. Lift the 2 loops with crochet hook and hold on hook—peg 1 is now empty. Lift the next 2 loops from peg 3 and place on the empty peg 1. Place the 2 loops on the crochet hook onto peg 3. You have now twisted the loops on peg 1 with loops on peg 3. Go to next peg with marker (peg 7) and lift the 2 loops onto crochet hook so that peg 7 is empty. Lift the loops on peg 9 and place them on the empty peg 7. Place the loops on crochet hook onto peg 9.

Do this twist with all the loops at the markers (see Instructions, page 102) with the adjacent right peg with loops and continue until all the twist stitches are complete. Push the sts down to the board. If the twist is too tight when you are working with it, try to work a tad bit looser with your wrapping.

INSTRUCTIONS

Cast on 64 sts in stockinette stitch, using contrasting color anchor yarn.

Adjust the sts on one side for the Open Rib stitch—this will also be the side for the cable twist. The opposite side will stay the same throughout afghan.

Place st markers on the 11 pegs where you will do the twist before you start to knit, using the knitting hook to lift the double loops and place the marker next to board then replace the loops. This will be on the 2-loop pegs 1, 7, 13, 19, 25, 31, 37, 43, 49, 55, and 61.

Work 6 rows in Open Rib, working cable twist on Row 6.

Work 4 rows in Open Rib, working Cable Twist in Row 4.

Rep this 4 row pattern throughout the afghan until you have completed 28–30 twist rows. Work Open Rib for 6 rows.

Bind off. Weave in ends.

Block.

FINISHING

To make the fringe, cut 12 in (30 cm) lengths of yarn. Use a crochet hook to attach two strands at a time to the ends of the throw to create a luxurious fringe.

Braid Circular Lapghan

Short row shaping makes this circular blanket possible. It is knit in wedges that are worked continuously, then when fifteen have been completed, the cast on edge is seamed to the bind-off edge. Finish with a decorative cable braid.

MATERIALS

Knitting loom

61–peg regular gauge knitting loom. All-n-One knitting loom is recommended for this project

Yarn

Approx 800 yards (730 m) bulky weight yarn. Sample shown in Berroco Comfort Chunky; Barley (A) x 3 skeins, Grape Jelly (B) x 2 skeins, and Aegean Sea (C) x 2 skeins

Gauge

7 sts x 12 rows = 2 in (5 cm) over stockinette stitch

Notions

Knitting tool, cable needle (for braid), tapestry needle, 19 stitch markers

Size

20 in (51 cm) wide

Abbreviations

For a list of common abbreviations see page 61
W&T   Lift the loop on the peg with stitch marker, e-wrap the peg, place loop back on peg

PATTERN NOTES

One strand throughout. Worked as a flat panel with short rows. Braid knitted separately and then sewn to the blanket.

INSTRUCTIONS

Place stitch markers on the following pegs: 3, 6, 9, 12, 15, 18, 21, 24, 27, 30, 33, 36, 39, 42, 45, 48, 51, 54, and 57).
Using A, cast on 61 sts.
Row 1: Purl to the end of the row.
*Row 2: Knit to last 4 sts, W on the peg with the stitch marker. W&T.
Row 3: Purl to the end of row.
Row 4: Knit to within 3 sts of the peg with the stitch marker. W on the peg with the stitch marker. W&T. Repeat rows 3–4 until only 4 stitches remain.
Next row: p4.*

There should be a pair of stitches between stitch markers all along the loom. The knitted fabric should resemble a pie-shaped panel.

Change to B, begin next wedge: Purl to the end of the row (The blanket is knit in short-row wedges that are worked continuously, then when fifteen wedges have been completed, the cast on edge is seamed to the bound off edge). Repeat from * to *.

Change to C, begin next wedge. Repeat from * to *.

Repeat last 3 wedges 4 more times for a total of 15 wedges.

Bind off with basic bind-off method.

Using mattress stitch, sew the cast-on edge to the bind-off edge. Run yarn through the hole at the center and pull closed.

Weave ends in and block.

Braid

Using A, cast on 8 sts.
Row 1: K3, c4b, k1.
Row 2: P1, k6, p1.
Row 3: K1, c4f, k3.
Row 4: P1, k6, p1.
Repeat rows 1–4 until braid measures 120 in (305 cm), or blanket circumference. Bind off with basic bind-off method.

FINISHING

Using mattress stitch, sew braid to outer edge of the blanket.

Embossed Diamonds Throw

Wrap yourself in comfort with this luxurious blanket worked in lovely merino wool.

MATERIALS

Knitting loom

Regular gauge, 193 peg. All-n-One knitting loom is recommended for this project

Yarn

Approx 1800 yards of worsted weight yarn. Sample shown in Debbie Bliss Cashmerino Aran; shade, Denim x 13 skeins

Notions

Knitting tool, tapestry needle

Gauge

18 sts x 20 rows = 4 in (10 cm) over stockinette stitch

Size

34 x 50 in (86 x 127 cm)

Abbreviations

For a list of common abbreviations see page 61

INSTRUCTIONS

Cast on 193 sts and prepare to work a flat panel.

Row 1: P1, k1, p1, *[k3, p1] twice, k1, p1; rep from * to end.
Row 2: K1, p1, *k3, p1, k1, p1, k3, p1; rep from * to last st, k1.
Row 3: K4, *[p1, k1] twice, p1, k5; rep from * to last 9 sts, [p1, k1] twice, p1, k4.
Row 4: K3, *[p1, k1] 3 times, p1, k3; rep from * to end.
Row 5: As row 3.
Row 6: As row 2.
Row 7: As row 1
Row 8: K1, p1, k1, *p1, k5, [p1, k1] twice; rep from * to end.
Row 9: [P1, k1] twice, *p1, k3 [p1, k1] 3 times; rep from * to last 9 sts, p1, k3, [p1, k1] twice, p1.
Row 10: As row 8.
Rep Rows 1–10 until panel measures 58 inches from cast-on edge.

Bind off loosely. Weave ends in.

Block to 46 x 30 in (117 x 76 cm).

Border

You will make 4 strips.

Cast on 15 sts and prepare to work a flat panel.

Row 1: *K1, p1; rep from * to last st, k1.
Row 2: *P1, k1; rep from * to last st, p1.

Rep Rows 1 and 2 until piece measures 49 in (125 cm).

Bind off loosely. Weave ends in.

Make a second piece measuring 49 in (125 cm) and third and fourth pieces each measuring 33 in (84 cm).

Block lightly.

FINISHING

Using mattress stitch, join borders to the blanket perimeter.

Weave ends in. Block lightly.

Aran Lapghan

A simple crossing of stitches make the design of this lapghan. The super soft wool yarn will provide you with a warm and cozy accessory.

MATERIALS

Knitting loom

100–peg regular gauge knitting loom. Sample was knit using a Décor Accents baby afghan loom

Yarn

Approx 600 yards bulky weight yarn. Sample shown in Malabrigo Chunky; color Tuareg x 6 skeins

Notions

Knitting tool, cable needle

Gauge

11 sts x 14 rows = 4 in (10 cm) over stockinette stitch

Size

30 x 40 in (76 x 102 cm)

Abbreviations

For a list of common abbreviations see page 61

PATTERN NOTES

Back cross purl (BCP)

Slip 1 stitch to cn and hold toward the center of the loom (peg is now empty), knit the next peg, then move this loop to the emptied peg, place the stitch from the cn on the empty peg then proceed to purl it.

Front cross purl (FCP)

Slip 1 stitch to cn and hold toward the front of the loom (peg is now empty), purl the next peg, then move this loop to the emptied peg, place the peg from the cn on the empty peg, proceed to knit it.

Hourglass stitch pattern

8	7	6	5	4	3	2	1	
●	●	●			●	●	●	**20**
	●	●	╱	⟨	⟨	╲	●	●	**19**
●	●			●	●		●	●	**18**
	●	╱	⟨	●	●	⟩	╲	**17**
●			●	●	●	●		●	**16**
	╱	⟨	●	●	●	●	⟩	╲	**15**
	●	●	●	●	●	●		**14**
	●	●	●	●	●	●		**13**
	●	●	●	●	●	●		**12**
⟨	╲	●	●	●	●	╱	⟨	**11**
●		●	●	●	●		●	**10**
●	⟩	╲	●	●	╱	⟨	●	**9**
●	●		●	●		●	●	**8**
●	●	⟨	╲	╱	⟨	●	●	**7**
●	●	●			●	●	●	**6**
●	●	●			●	●	●	**5**

●	Purl RS: purl stitch
(blank)	Knit RS: knit stitch
╱ ⟨	BCP: see notes
⟩ ╲	FCP: see notes

INSTRUCTIONS

Cast on 100 sts. Prepare to work a flat panel.

Row 1: Knit.
Row 2: Purl.
Row 3: Knit.
Row 4: Purl.
Rows 5, 7, 9, 11, 13, 15, 17, 19: K2, follow Hourglass Stitch Pattern to last 2 sts, k2.
Rows 6, 8, 10, 12, 14, 16, 18, 20: P2, follow Hourglass Stitch Pattern to last 2 sts, p2.

Repeat rows 5–20 until item measures 38 in (96 cm) from cast-on edge.
Next row: Purl.
Next row: Knit.
Next row: Purl.

Bind off with basic bind off method.

Weave ends in and block to measurements.

Simple Afghan Throw

This simple throw can be knitted in a few evenings but will keep you toasty warm through the long winter months.

MATERIALS

Knitting loom

Regular gauge, 198 peg, Sample made on the Super Afghan Loom

Yarn

Approx 1300 yards of worsted weight yarn. Sample shown in Lion Brand Heartland; shade, Olympic x 6 skeins

Notions

Knitting tool, tapestry needle

Gauge

9 sts x 21 rows = 2 in (5 cm) over stockinette stitch

Size

44 x 56 in (112 x 142 cm)

Abbreviations

For a list of common abbreviations see page 61

INSTRUCTIONS

Cast on 198 sts and prepare to work a flat panel.

Row 1: Knit.
Row 2: Purl.
Rows 3-10: Rep rows 1 and 2.
Row 11: Knit.
Row 12: P5, k to last 5 pegs, p5.

Rep Rows 11 and 12 until panel measures 55 in (140 cm) from cast-on edge.

Work the next 9 rows as follows:

Rep Rows 1 and 2 a further 4 times then work Row 1 once more.

Bind off loosely. Weave in ends. Block.

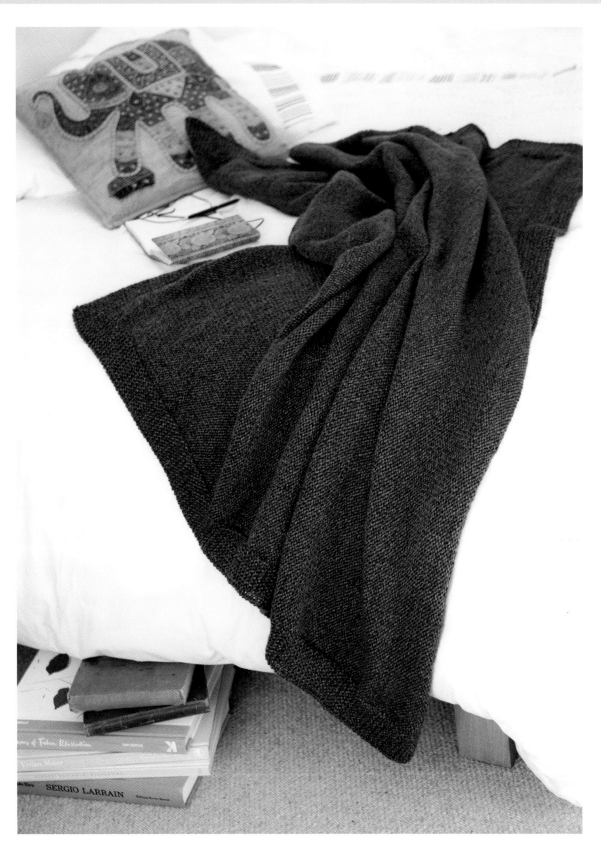

Just a Little Throw

Everyone loves simple, easy-care afghans for the home or as gifts for friends and family. They are always comforting and welcome when found lying on your bed or sofa. With a few basic stitch variations, this afghan is great for a beginner wanting to make warm, cozy afghans in beautiful double knit.

MATERIALS

Knitting loom

28 inch Knitting Board + peg extenders by Authentic Knitting Board; blanket requires 64 double stitches, 1cm spacer

Yarn

Approx 1100 yards of worsted/ heavy worsted weight machine washable yarn. Sample shown in Rowan Lima; shade: Guatemala x 10 skeins

Notions

Knitting hook, crochet hook

Gauge

12 sts x 16 rows = 4 in (10cm) over stockinette stitch

Size

26 x 30 in (66 x 76 cm)

Abbreviations

For a list of common abbreviations see page 61 See page 88 for instructions for working Figure-8 stitch

INSTRUCTIONS

Set up loom to double knit with 1cm spacer.

Using Figure-8 stitch, cast on 64 sts.

Work 4 rows in Figure-8 stitch.

*Work 6 rows in stockinette stitch.

Work 6 rows in k1, p1 rib.

Work 4 rows in Figure-8 stitch.*

Rep the 16 rows from * to * 8 times or until your afghan measures 21 x 32 in (54 x 81 cm).

Bind off loosely.

Weave in ends.

Block to 26 x 30 in (66 x 76 cm).

FINISHING

Cut 128 lengths of yarn each 7 in (18 cm) long. Place a crochet hook through each Figure-8 st and place center of a length of yarn on hook. Pull the yarn through the st then pull the tail through the loop. Pull snugly. Rep for each end st.

PART FOUR
Bed Covers

Sampler Block Bedspread

This bedspread is worked in individual squares making it a great project for on-the-go. All the squares are worked in a combination of knit and purl making it ideal for a beginner to try out new stitch patterns.

MATERIALS

Knitting loom

Regular gauge, 48 peg. Sample made using the All-n-One loom

Yarn

3200 yards of worsted weight yarn. Sample shown in Cascade Superwash 220; shades: Aran, Citron, Silver Gray, Sunset Orange, Blue Horizon, Strawberry Pink, Denim, Cotton Candy, and Midnight Heather x 2 skeins of each

Notions

Knitting tool, tapestry needle, crochet hook US size J/10 (6 mm)

Gauge

20 sts x 34 rows = 4 in (10 cm) over stockinette stitch

Size

72 x 72 in (196 x 196 cm)

Abbreviations

For a list of common abbreviations see page 61

wyif   With yarn held at front of work

wyif sl   lift loop off peg, run working yarn behind peg, replace lifted loop onto peg

PATTERN NOTES

You will be creating 81 x 8 in (20 cm) squares in total; 9 squares of each of the 9 stitch patterns. The squares are then seamed together to create the bedspread. To make the squares easier to stitch together, an HS stitch was added to both sides of each square (these are not listed in the pattern).

The finished squares will be different sizes, but if you wet block them (see page 52) to the same size, then steam iron them, they will be equal in size.

To aid seaming, you can add an extra HS edge stitch to each side of each square (these stitches are not included in the pattern instructions).

INSTRUCTIONS

Moss stitch square (make 9 squares using color Aran)

Cast on 48 sts and prepare to work a flat panel.

Rows 1 and 2: *K2, p2; rep from * to end
Rows 3 and 4: *P2, k2; rep from * to end

Rep Rows 1–4 until panel measures approx. 5 in (12.75 cm) from cast-on edge. (The sample required 14

repeats and a k row before binding off.)

Bind off leaving a 12 in (30 cm) tail to use for seaming.

Simple basketweave (make 9 squares using color Citron)

Cast on 48 sts and prepare to work a flat panel.

Row 1: Knit
Rows 2, 4, 6: *K4, p4; rep from * to end
Rows 3, 5: *P4, k4; rep from * to end
Row 7: Knit
Rows 8, 10, 12: *P4, k4; rep from * to end
Rows 9, 11: *K4, p4; rep from * to end

Rep Rows 1–12 until panel measures approx. 5½ in (14 cm) from cast-on edge. (The sample required 5 repeats and an additional Row 1 before binding off.)

Bind off leaving a 12 in (30 cm) tail to use for seaming.

Big bamboo (make 9 squares using color Silver Gray)

Cast on 36 sts and prepare to work a flat panel.

Rows 1, 3, 7, and 9: *P2, k4; rep from * to end

Rows 2, 4, 8, 10: *K4, p2; rep from * to end

Row 5: *P8, k4; rep from * to end

Row 6: *K4, p8; rep from * to end

Row 11: P2, *k4, p8; rep from * to last 6 sts, p6

Row 12: P6, *k4, p8; rep from * to last 2 sts, p2

Rep Rows 1–12 until panel measures approx. 5½ in (14 cm) from cast-on edge. (The sample required 4 repeats before binding off.)

Bind off leaving a 12 in (30 cm) tail to use for seaming.

Rib and welt pattern (make 9 squares using color Sunset Orange)

Cast on 32 sts and prepare to work a flat panel. (The sample required 1 k row before starting the pattern repeat.)

Row 1: *K1, p1, k1, p5; rep from * to end.

Row 2: *P5, k1, p1, k1; rep from * to end.

Row 3: K1, p1, *k5, p1, k1, p1; to from * to last 6 sts, k5, p1.

Row 4: P1, k5, *p1, k1, p1, k5; rep from * to last 2 sts p1, k1.

Row 5: K1, *p5, k1, p1, k1; rep from * to last 7 sts, p5, k1, p1.

Row 6: P1, k1, p5, *k1, p1, k1, p5; rep from * to last st, k1.

Row 7: *K5, p1, k1, p1; rep from * to end.

Row 8: *P1, k1, p1, k5; rep from * to end.

Row 9: P4, *k1, p1, k1, p5; to last 4 sts, [k1, p1] twice.

Row 10: [P1, k1] twice, *p5, k1, p1, k1; rep from * to last 4 sts, p4.

Row 11: K3, *p1, k1, p1, k5; to last 5 sts, p1, k1, p1, k2.

Row 12: K2, p1, k1, p1, *k5, p1, k1, p1; rep from * to last 3 sts, k3.

Row 13: P2, *k1, p1, k1, p5*; rep from * to last 6 sts, k1, p1, k1, p3.

Row 14: P3, k1, p1, k1, *p5, k1, p1, k1; rep from * to last 2 sts, p2.

Row 15: K1, *p1, k1, p1, k5; rep from * to last 7 sts, p1, k1, p1, k4.

Row 16: K4, p1, k1, p1, *k5, p1, k1, p1; rep from * to last st, k1.

Rep rows 1–16 until panel measures approx. 6 in (15 cm) from cast-on edge. (The sample required 4 repeats before binding off.)

Bind off leaving a 12 in (30 cm) tail to use for seaming.

Linen ridge stitch (make 9 squares using color Blue Horizon)

Cast on 32 sts and prepare to work a flat panel.

Row 1: Knit.

Row 2: K1, *sl1 wyif, k1; rep from * to last st, k1.

Row 3: Knit.

Row 4: K1, *k1, sl1 wyif; rep from * to last st, k1.

Rep rows 1–4 until panel measures approx. 6 in (15 cm) from cast-on edge. (The sample required 17 repeats plus additional rows 1–3 before binding off.)

Bind off using the basic bind off (see page 28) and leaving a 12 in (30 cm) tail to use for seaming.

Note: The right side of the square is the reverse working side).

Stockinette stitch (make 9 squares using color Strawberry Pink)

Cast on 34 sts and prepare to work a flat panel.

Row 1: Knit to the end.

Rep Row 1 until panel measures approx. 5½ in (14 cm) from cast-on edge.

Bind off using the basic bind off and leaving a 12 in (30 cm) tail to use for seaming.

Garter stitch (make 9 squares using color Denim)

Cast on 32 sts and prepare to work a flat panel.

874	886	873	891	818	841	819	888	872
886	873	891	818	841	819	888	872	874
873	891	818	841	819	888	872	874	886
891	818	841	819	888	872	874	886	873
818	841	819	888	872	874	886	873	891
841	819	888	872	874	886	873	891	818
819	888	872	874	886	873	891	818	841
888	872	874	886	873	891	818	841	819
872	874	886	873	891	818	841	819	888

LEGEND

Aran

Citron

Silver Gray

Sunset Orange

Blue Horizon

Strawberry Pink

Denim

Cotton Candy

Midnight Heather

Row 1: Knit to the end.
Row 2: Purl to the end.

Rep Row 1 and Row 2 until the panel measures approx. 4½ in (11.5 cm) from cast-on edge.

Bind off using the basic bind off and leaving a 12 in (30 cm) tail to use for seaming.

Triangles (make 9 squares using color Cotton Candy)

Cast on 32 sts and prepare to work a flat panel.

Row 1: P to the end.
Row 2: *K1, p7; rep from * to the end.
Row 3: *P6, k2; rep from * to the end.
Row 4: *K 3, p5; rep from * to the end.
Row 5: *P 4, k4; rep from * to the end.
Row 6: *K 5, p3; rep from * to the end.
Row 7: *P 2, k6; rep from * to the end.
Row 8: *K 7, p1; rep from * to the end.

Rep Rows 1–8 until panel measures approx. 6 in (15 cm) from cast-on edge. (The sample required 6 repeats.)

Bind off using the basic bind off and leaving a 12 in (30 cm) tail to use for seaming.

Roman stitch (make 9 squares using color Midnight Heather)

Cast on 34 sts and prepare to work a flat panel.

Rows 1, 2, 3, 4: Knit.
Rows 5 and 6: *K1, p1; rep from * to end.

Rep Rows 1–6 until panel measures approx. 6½ in (16.5 cm) from cast-on edge. (The sample required 11 repeats plus an additional rows 1–3.)

Bind off using the basic bind off and leaving a 12 in (30 cm) tail to use for seaming.

ASSEMBLY

Wet-block all the blocks to 8 in (20 cm) square. Steam iron once dry. Using the layout below, seam the squares together using mattress stitch. Weave ends in. Block lightly again.

BORDER

Work a single crochet border around the entire afghan with your colors of choice. Weave ends in.

Cables & Lace Throw

Lace with a touch of seed stitch surround small cables throughout this lovely afghan. The border is worked separately in an accent color, work it in the same color as the body of the blanket for a more subtle look.

MATERIALS

Knitting loom

188 pegs, regular gauge. Sample was knit using Super Afghan knitting loom by Knitting Board.

Yarn

1300 yards in worsted weight yarn. Sample was worked in Cascade 220; shades Feather Gray (MC) x 7 skeins and Chocolate (CC) x 2 skeins

Notions

Knitting tool, tapestry needle, cable needle

Gauge

18 stitches x 32 rows = 4 in (10 cm) over stockinette stitch

Size

50 x 60 in (127 x 152 cm)

Abbreviations

For a list of common abbreviations see page 61
YO   Yarn over
K2tog Knit two stitches together
4st LC 4 stitch left cross cable
         (see page 41)

INSTRUCTIONS

Using MC, cast on 188 pegs, prepare to work a flat panel.
Row 1: P1, k1, p1, yo, k2tog, p1, k1, p1, *4st LC, p1, k1, p1, yo, k2tog, p1, k1, p1; rep from * to end.
Row 2: K1, p1, k4, p1, k1, *k5, p1, k4, p1, k1; rep from * to end.
Row 3: P1, k1, p1, k2tog, yo, p1, k1, p1, *k4, p1, k1, p1, k2tog, yo, p1, k1, p1; rep from * to end.
Row 4: As row 2.
Row 5: P1, k1, p1, yo, k2tog, p1, k1, p1, *4st RC, p1, k1, p1, yo, k2tog, p1, k1, p1; rep from * to end.
Row 6: As row 2.
Row 7: P1, k1, p1, k2tog, yo, p1, k1, p1, *k4, p1, k1, p1, k2tog, yo, p1, k1, p1; rep from * to end.
Row 8: As row 2.

Repeat Rows 1–8 until piece measures 56 in (142 cm) long.

Bind off loosely. Weave ends in.

Block to 47 x 58 in (120 x 147 cm).

Border

You will make 4 strips.

Using CC, cast on 13 sts, prepare to work a flat panel.
Row 1: *K1, p1; rep from * to last st, k1.
Row 2: *P1, k1; rep from * to last st, p1.

Repeat Row 1 and Row 2 until piece measures 48 in (122 cm). Make a second strip in the same way.

Make 2 more strips in the same way, but 58 in (148 cm) long.

FINISHING

Seam borders to throw using mattress stitch. Weave in ends.

Block throw.

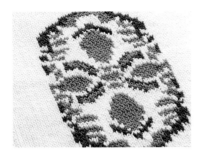

Summer Rose Bed Afghan

This beautiful queen size afghan is worked in nine sections with borders between each section and one large center medallion in multiple colors. It adds that special something to your full or queen size bed.

MATERIALS

Knitting loom

28 inch Knitting Board + peg extenders by Authentic Knitting Board

Yarn

4800 yards of bulky weight yarn. Sample shown in Schachemayr Extra Merino Big; shades: (MC) Cream x 45 skeins, (CC1) Lipstick Pink x 13 skeins, (CC2) Olive Heather x 1 skein

Notions

Knitting hook, crochet hook US size H/8 (5 mm) or J/10 (6 mm), large tapestry needle

Gauge

14 sts x 20 rows = 4 in (10 cm) over stockinette stitch

Size

58 x 88 in (147 x 224 cm)

Abbreviations

For a list of common abbreviations see page 61

PATTERN NOTES

Blanket requires 64 double stitches or full board, 1cm spacer (or the smallest setting of the little wood spacers).

Afghan is worked in 9 sections labeled A, B, C and D. Each section measures approx. 19 x 29 in (48 x 74 cm).

Each section has a border on either 2, 3, or 4 sides designated as:

(B) Bottom Edge, (T) Top edge, (L) Left edge—beginning of row, (R) Right edge—end of row.

Borders are always 6 sts for L and R; 8 rows for T and B.

Set up your loom to work in double knit using the 1cm spacer.

Be sure you work the 3 sections simultaneously so they all have the same number of rows. Your yarns may get a bit twisted around each other. Just stop every so often and straighten them out. If you work without doing the color twist, you will need to sew the border to the main body when you are done with the piece. Either method is acceptable.

Knit	QTY	How Many Sides	Where
A	2	3	L, B, T
B	2	3	L, B, R
C	4	2	L, B (one piece includes center design)
D	1	4	L, B, T, R

WORKING THE CHART:

When working the chart, start at the bottom with row 1 reading across from right to left. Work row 2 reading from left to right. Mark off each row as you go to keep track of where you are.

When working a color stitch, weave it from front to back on each st needed then lay the yarn aside until needed again. Be sure to carry it between the rows of pegs so that it does not show in finished afghan. After you work across a row with CC1 and CC2, finish the row in MC. You will skip over the pegs with the color yarns while maintaining stockinette pattern.

Work with small lengths of colored yarn on bobbins, rather than try to string one skein all the way across the sections where there is no color. Do not carry the yarns behind more than 3 or 4 pegs at a time. You may need up to 6 colored bobbins at a time.

Knit the color work rows loosely to make sure that the knit stitches are thick enough from the front side to cover all the carried strands.

Lay the carried strands between the two boards of pegs, with absolutely no tension on that part of the yarn, so that the colored stitches are not pulled out of place from the front side.

You could add more colored panels to the design, if desired. Or make matching pillow shams with the rose pattern on them.

Your design consists of 30 sts across and 60 rows. At widest point of the design, your section will have 6 sts of (L) border, 14 sts of solid color (M), 30 sts of design, 14 sts of solid color for a total of 64 pegs/sts. Mark the central 30 sts so you will always know where the design will be. You may want to mark the center of loom also—a little piece of colored tape will do. Your tape will cover the loom from peg #21 thru #51. Let's clarify this one more way:

Looking at the graph of the medallion, row #1 is bottom of graph. You will work the 30 sts of design starting on lower left corner, after the (P) border and solid color (42 rows) are complete.

Row 43: (12) MC, (1) CC2, (4) CC1, (1) CC2, (12) MC—DESIGN ONLY.
Row 44: (10) MC, (2) CC2, (6) CC1, (2) CC2, (10) MC—DESIGN ONLY.

Remember you will have the (L) border and MC area before doing the 30 sts of design area. So, your complete section, (64) pegs, will follow this:

Row 43: (6) CC1, (26) MC, (1) olive, (4) CC1, (1) CC2, (26) MC—

FULL ROW.
Row 44: (6) CC1, (24) MC, (2) olive, (6) CC1, (2) CC2, (24) MC—FULL ROW.

Continue working up the graph from bottom to top until all 60 rows of design are complete. Then continue working the remaining rows for this (c) panel.

INSTRUCTIONS:
Section A (make 2 alike)
Using CC1, cast on 64 sts. Lay anchor yarn.

Work 8 rows in stockinette stitch.

Row 9: Continue in stockinette and work 6 sts. Tie on MC, leaving CC1 attached, work in MC to end of row. All following rows will work both color sections. Where the 2 sections meet, be sure to twist the yarns so the sections stay connected.

Continue as set until you have completed 128 rows.

Cut MC leaving a 5 inch tail and knot. Lay it across the sts.

Work 8 CC1 rows for T-border. Piece should measure approx. 39 in (99 cm).

Bind off using the loose, 2-loop crochet method.

Section B (make 3 alike)
Using CC1, cast on 64 sts. Lay anchor yarn.

Work 8 rows in stockinette.

Row 9: Continue in stockinette and work 6 sts. Tie on MC, leaving CC1 attached, work in MC to last 6 sts. Tie on a second skein of CC1 and work last 6 sts in stockinette. You work the 3 sections separately and it is important to twist the yarns together at each color change.

Continue as set until you have completed 136 rows or until the piece measures 34 in (86 cm).

Cut all yarns and knot.

Bind off using the loose, 2-loop crochet method.

Section C (make 3 alike and 1 with medallion design)

Note: Work from chart for the center medallion design incorporating it into the instructions set below

Using CC1, cast on 64 sts. Lay anchor yarn.

Work 8 rows in stockinette.

Row 9: Continue in stockinette and work 6 sts. Tie on MC, leaving CC1 attached, work in MC to end

of row. in stockinette. All following rows will work both color sections. Where the 2 sections meet, be sure to twist the yarns so the sections stay connected.

Continue as set until you have completed all 136 rows. Cut all yarns and knot.

Bind off using the loose, 2-loop crochet method.

Section D (make 1)
Using CC1, cast on 64 sts. Lay anchor yarn.

Work 8 rows in stockinette.

Row 9: Continue in stockinette and work 6 sts. Tie on MC, leaving CC1 attached, work in MC to last 6 sts. Tie on a second skein of CC1 and work last 6 sts in stockinette. You work the 3 sections separately and it is important to twist the yarns together at each color change.

Continue as set until you have completed 128 rows.

Cut MC leaving a 5 inch tail and knot. Lay it across the sts. Cut the second CC1 skein at R side and knot.

Work 8 CC1 rows for T-border.

Bind off using the loose, 2-loop crochet method.

FINISHING
Lay the 9 sections out to complete the design. All sections should be going in same direction with a border around each section and the entire afghan.

Sew the sections together using an invisible stitch in either MC or CC1, but when connecting 2 borders use CC1. Start by connecting the top 3 sections – 2 x A and 1 x D at top right edge.

Next, connect the 3 central sections – 1 x C, 1 x C with central medallion, 1 x B.

Now, connect the bottom 3 sections – 2 x C and 1 x B.

Finally, connect the 3 x 3 section units to complete the design. Take care to match the corners and edges so there are no holes and so they lay flat.

Once complete, you may want to work a single crochet edge around entire afghan with CC1 or CC2 to stabilize it.

Striped Mitered Square Blanket

The geometric squares of this blanket are reminiscent of patchwork.

MATERIALS

Knitting loom

Regular gauge, 50 pegs. Sample made on the Sock Loom 2

Yarn

Approx 3700 yards of worsted weight yarn. Shown in Rowan Pure Wool Aran; shade: (MC) Sage x 4 skeins and (CC) Mid Indigo x 4 skeins

Notions

Knitting tool, tapestry needle, crochet hook US size I/9 (5.5 mm)

Gauge

9 sts x 18 rows = 2 in (5 cm) over stockinette stitch

Size

36 x 46 in (92 x 117 cm)

Abbreviations

For a list of common abbreviations see page 61

PATTERN NOTES

Start with MC, then switch colors every four rows. Do not cut yarns, simply carry them along the side loosely and without adding any tension, when not in use. Also, make sure to work each side's turning peg stitches loosely to ensure an even sided square.

Each square is approx. 6 x 8 in (15 x 20 cm).

INSTRUCTIONS

Mitered Squares (Make 30)
With MC, Cast on 50 sts and prepare to knit a flat panel.

Row 1: K23, (k2tog) twice, k23. Slide the slider inwards.
Row 2: Purl.
Row 3: K22, (k2tog) twice, k22. Slide the slider inwards.
Row 4: Purl.

Join CC, and continue with the pattern.

Rep the last two rows, dec 2 sts every odd numbered row, until 2 sts remain.

Note: On every odd numbered row, the "k" numbers will go down by 1 from k22 to k21 to k20 etc right down to k1.

Final row: K2tog.

Bind off leaving a 10 in (25 cm) tail of both yarns to use for seaming.

FINISHING

Block all the squares prior to seaming.
Use the layout below to arrange your squares, seam the squares together using mattress stitch.

Weave ends in. Block.

Border

Stabilize the blanket by working a single crochet border around the edges.

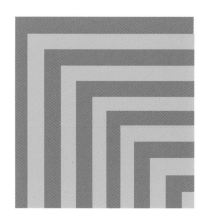

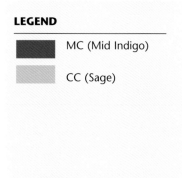

LEGEND

▮ MC (Mid Indigo)

▯ CC (Sage)

BLANKET LAYOUT

PART FIVE

Resources

Quick reference guide to looms

Large gauge knitting looms

Distance from center of peg to center of peg: ¾ in (2 cm)

Available in: wood & plastic, with nylon pegs, plastic, wood, and metal

Yarn: Bulky-weight yarns or 2 strands of medium-weight yarn

Knits: Bulky-weight knits and knits that will be felted

Loom Gauge: Approximately 1½–2 stitches per 1 in (2.5 cm)

Compared to needle knitting stitch gauge: size 13 (9 mm)

Regular gauge knitting looms

Distance from center of peg to center of peg: ½ in (1.2 cm)

Available in: wood & plastic, with nylon pegs, plastic, wood, and metal

Yarn: Chunky-weight yarns or 2 strands of sport-weight yarn

Knits: Medium-weight knits

Gauge: Approximately 3–3.5 stitches per 1 in (2.5 cm)

Compared to needle knitting stitch gauge: size 10 (6 mm)

Small gauge knitting looms

Distance from center of peg to center of peg: ⅜ to 3⁄7 in

Available in: wood & plastic, with nylon pegs, plastic, wood, and metal

Yarn: Worsted-weight/medium-weight yarn

Knits: Medium and light weight knits

Gauge: Approximately 3.5–4 stitches per 1 in (2.5 cm)

Compared to needle knitting stitch gauge: size 7–8 (4.5–5 mm)

Fine gauge knitting looms

Distance from center of peg to center of peg: ¼ ins

Available in: wood base and metal pins/pegs

Yarn: Sports-weight/worsted

Knits: Light-weight knits

Gauge: Approximately 4–5 stitches per 1 in (2.5 cm)

Compared to needle knitting stitch Gauge: Size 5–6 (3.75–4 mm)

Extra fine gauge knitting looms

Distance from center of peg to center of peg: 3⁄16 in

Available in: wood base and metal pins/pegs

Yarn: Fingering-weight/sock-weight

Knits: Light-weight knits

Gauge: Approximately 7–8 stitches per 1 in (2.5 cm)

Compared to needle knitting stitch gauge: size 1.5–2 (2.25–2.75 mm)

Washing your knits

Hand-washing is the best washing technique for all your knitted items. Even those items that were knitted with machine-washable yarns can have their life extended by practicing good washing habits.

Use pure soap flakes or special wool soap. Wash and rinse your item gently in warm water. Maintain an even water temperature; changing water temperature can shock your wool items and accidentally felt them. Before washing, test for colorfastness. If the yarn bleeds, wash the item in cold water. If the yarn is colorfast, wash with warm water.

Fill a basin or sink with water, add the soap flakes or wool soap, and using your hands, gently wash the knitted item. Avoid rubbing, unless you want your item to matt the yarn and felt it together.

To rinse, empty the basin and fill with clean warm water, immerse your knitted item and gently squeeze out all the soap suds. Repeat until all the soap suds are gone and the water is soap free. Pat as much of the water out as you can; use the palms of your hands. Do not wring your item as this may cause wrinkles and distort the yarn. Place the knitted item between two towels and squeeze as much of the water out as you can.

To dry your item, lay it flat away from direct sunlight; block again if necessary to match measurements.

Glossary

Anchor peg
The side peg on a knitting loom. Some knitting looms have a peg or thumb tack at the base of the loom. It can be used to anchor the yarn.

Bind off
Taking the item off the knitting loom. Knitting the very last row.

Blocking
The process of laying the knitted pieces flat on a surface, wetting them and giving them their shape.

Casting on
The process of setting up the very first row. It becomes the foundation row of your knitted item.

Double stitch
A variation of the single stitch. Loom must have 2 loops on each peg to start knitting the double stitch. Take yarn toward the inside of the knitting loom, wrap around the peg in a counter-clockwise direction. Lift the bottommost strand off the peg.

Gauge
Also known as knitting tension, this is the number of stitches and rows to a given width and length. The size of each stitch varies depending on the yarn, the knitting loom gauge and the loom knitter's tension.

Graft
Join two edges together invisibly.

Knit stitch
One of the foundation stitches. The knit stitch is made by placing the working yarn above the loop on the peg, inserting your knitting tool from the bottom up through the loop on the peg and catching the working

yarn. Pull the working yarn through the loop on the peg. Take the loop off the peg and place the newly formed loop on the peg.

Knitting over (KO)
The process of forming a stitch. To knit over, you need to lift off one (or more) of the loops on the peg and let it fall off toward the center of the knitting loom.

Loom gauge
The measurement from peg to peg. Usually measured from the center of the next adjacent peg. Gauges range from extra fine ($\frac{3}{16}$ in/2 mm) to extra large (¾ in/2 cm).

Mattress stitch
The process of joining two pieces of knitted fabric together.

Purl stitch
One of the foundation stitches. Purl stitch is done by placing the working yarn below the loop on the peg, insert your knitting tool from the top down through the loop on the peg, catch the working yarn. Pull the working yarn through the loop on the peg. Take the loop off the peg and place the newly formed loop on the peg.

Rib stitch
A stitch that is formed by combining knits and purls.

Running stitch
A series of small, even hand-sewing stitches.

Seaming
The process of joining two pieces of knitted fabric together.

Short-row

A technique used in shaping, it adds rows to a segment of the knitted piece. Often used in loom knitting for shaping the heel and toe section of a sock.

Single stitch

The Single Stitch is done by wrapping around the peg in the e-wrap method. Loom must have one loop on each peg to start knitting the single stitch. Take yarn toward the inside of the knitting loom, wrap around the peg in a counter-clockwise direction. Lift the bottommost strand off the peg.

Slip knot

A knot that is placed on the first peg. It becomes the first stitch.

Stockinette stitch

The smooth side of a knitted fabric. It resembles small Vs. Formed by knitting the knit stitch or twisted knit stitch or twisted knit stitch on every single row.

Tail end

The yarn that remains at the end of your knitted project.

Weave in ends

When the knitted item is completed, you need to hide all the yarn tail ends. You weave the yarn tail ends into the wrong side of the item.

Working yarn

The yarn coming from the yarn skein that is being used to knit on the knitting loom.

Suppliers

Knitting Looms

You can find a large variety of looms on the internet.

Authentic Knitting Board
www.knittingboard.com
60 Carysbrook Road
Fork Union, VA 23055
Décor Accents, Inc.

Provo Craft
www.provocraft.com
151 East 3450 North
Spanish Fork, UT 84660

Blocking wires

Take it Personally
www.giftsbytip.com

Yarns

Berroco, Inc.
www.berroco.com
14 Elmdale Rd.
PO Box 367
Uxbridge, MA 01569

Cascade
www.cascadeyarns.com

KnitPicks
www.knitpicks.com
13118 NE 4th Street Vancouver, WA 98684

Knitting Fever, Inc.
www.knittingfever.com
P.O. Box 502
Roosevelt, NY 11575
(Distributors of Rowan, Debbie Bliss, and Noro yarns)

Lion Brand Yarns
www.lionbrand.com
135 Kero Road
Carlstadt, NJ 07072
(Distributors of Lion Brand and Martha Stewart yarns)

Malabrigo
www.malabrigoyarn.com

Patons
www.patonsyarns.com
PO Box 40
Listowel, ON N4W 3H3
Canada
(Distributors of Schachemayer yarns)

Premier Yarns
www.premieryarns.com
5991 Caldwell Park Drive
Harrisburg, NC 28075

Index

Acknowledgments

I would like to express a sincere heartfelt thank you to all the sample knitters who contributed countless hours of work to produce the lovely samples for this book project. Without their help, the production of this book would not have been feasible.

I would like to express my gratitude to my family and their support throughout the years with my loom knitting endeavors. The three of them, my husband and two children, are always there supporting me, helping me with my ideas. A special hug to my extended family for always believing in me and for cheering me on each time I share my news about a new book.

A special thank you to my friend Pat Novak for her invaluable help in the double knitting section of the book; her ample knowledge on the subject made the addition of double knitting a great asset to the book.

With much gratitude, I would like to thank Graciela Worth for her help with the Entrelac Baby Blanket. Graciela was the original "translator" of entrelac to the knitting looms and her work inspired this baby blanket.

Lastly, thank you to all my loom knitting friends—thank you for supporting our craft throughout the years.

Contributors

Pat Novak, designed the double knitted patterns in this book. She is a designer and pattern developer of double knit, and has worked on knitting boards for over 15 years after more than 20 years knitting with knitting needles. She has taught double knit techniques in classes around the US.

I would like to thank the following knitters for their invaluable help in knitting the afghans, blankets, and throws for this book: Natalie Burxtyn, Christy Cannon, Dee Ann Dodson, Bethany Dailey, Megan Dailey, Knitty Fred, Tricia Roberts, Wendy Stellwag, Alyna Waters, Janet Wilfang, and Charity Windham.

The publishers would like to thank the following companies for generously supplying yarns for use in this book: Knitting Fever (Designer Yarns), Lion Brand Yarns, Patons, Premier Yarns, Cascade and Malabrigo.